P9-DYD-756

SCHOLASTIC

PURPOSEFUL
CONFERENCES
Powerful Writing!

Strategies, Tips, and Teacher-Student Dialogues
for Helping Kids Improve Their Writing

Marilyn Pryle

New York • Toronto • London • Auckland • Sydney
Mexico City • New Delhi • Hong Kong • Buenos Aires

Teaching *Resources*

For Tim, who gives me a room of my own

ACKNOWLEDGMENTS

I am again grateful to the students of East Middle School in Braintree, Massachusetts, and the administration of the Braintree Public Schools, especially Michael Connelly, Ann Keenan, and Mary Cunningham, for having the vision to make time for Writing Workshop. I also thank Virginia Dooley for entrusting me with this project, and Mary Beth Booth for her reading and advice. Finally, I am grateful for my family's love and support, especially from Tiernan and Gavin, my two small wordsmiths.

Scholastic Inc. grants permission to photocopy the reproducible pages from this book for classroom and home use. No other part of this publication may be reproduced in whole or in part, or stored in a retrieval system, without written permission of the publisher. For information regarding permission, write to Scholastic Inc., 557 Broadway, New York, NY 10012.

Cover design by Brian LaRossa
Cover photo by www.jupiterimages.com
Interior design by Sarah Morrow
Author photo by Joshua Jury

ISBN-13: 978-0-545-01117-4
ISBN-10: 0-545-01117-5

Copyright © 2009 by Marilyn Pryle
Published by Scholastic Inc. All rights reserved.
Printed in the U.S.A.

1 2 3 4 5 6 7 8 9 10   40   15 14 13 12 11 10 09

CONTENTS

INTRODUCTION 5

   About the Book 6

CHAPTER 1 ✳ **Behind the Scenes of a Conference** 7

   Classroom Organization 7

   Workshop Procedure 8

   Silence 8

   Topics for Writing 9

CHAPTER 2 ✳ **General Conference Guidelines** 10

   Frequency 10

   Location 11

   Duration 11

   Content 12

CHAPTER 3 ✳ **"I Don't Have Anything to Write"** 14

   Autobiography • *Brainstorming for Topics* 14

CHAPTER 4 ✳ **Only Bones: Generating Details** 18

   Autobiography • *Using the Five Senses; Taking Notes in the Field* 18

CHAPTER 5 ✳ **Searching for Meaning: Cultivating Theme** 25

   Autobiography • *Finding Theme* 27

   Autobiography • *Developing Theme* 29

   Character Sketch • *Weaving In Theme* 33

     Also: Dependent Clauses, Tense Consistency

   Process Essay • *Finding Theme in an Expository Essay* 38

CHAPTER 6 ✳ **Jumbled Ideas: Instilling Organization** 40

   Personal Essay • *Major Cutting and Rearranging of Ideas* 41

     Also: Adding Sensory Details; Developing Theme

   Persuasive Essay • *Minor Trimming and Moving of Ideas* 46

     Also: Sharpening a Thesis

CHAPTER 7 ✳ **Finishing Strong: Conclusions and Clinchers** 53

   Autobiography • *Using an Image as an Ending* 54

     Also: Linking Verbs

Persuasive Essay • *Using Imagery and a Complex Sentence*. 56
Personal Essay • *Revising a Weak Question Into a Strong Statement* 57

CHAPTER 8 ✳ **Grabbing the Reader: Introductions** 63
Autobiography • *Starting With a Detail*. 64
    Also: Strengthening Verbs
Persuasive Essay • *Starting With a Question* 66
    Also: Eradicating Linking Verbs
Historical Fiction • *Starting With a Quotation* 69
    Also: Using Strong Verbs
Short Story Analysis • *Starting With a General Statement of Truth* 73
    Also: Developing a Thesis
Autobiography • *Using Sensory Detail and Flashback* 75
    Also: Using the Past Perfect Tense

CHAPTER 9 ✳ **Using the Best Words** 82
Persuasive Essay • *Replacing Banned Words* 84
Persuasive Essay • *Strengthening Weak Words* 86
Autobiography • *Revising Clichés* 87
Book Review • *Condensing Weak Verbs*. 90
Character Sketch • *Changing Linking Verbs to Actions* 92
Analysis of a Poem • *Eradicating Linking Verbs by Combining Sentences* 95
    Also: Honing a Thesis
Introductory Letter • *Converting Passive Voice to Active* 97

CHAPTER 10 ✳ **What to Call It: Finding Titles** 101
Autobiography • *Using Theme and Imagery* 101
Persuasive Essay • *Using the Thesis*. 104

CHAPTER 11 ✳ **Talking to Students About Poetry** 106
Free Verse • *Sharpening Details; Using a Simile for an Ending; Strengthening Line Breaks*. . 108
Free Verse • *Cutting Words* 114
Ode • *Using Imagery to Establish Mood; Changing Clichés; Finding an Ending* 118
    Also: Using Consistent Verb Tense
Rhymed Poem • *Revising Forced Rhymes*. 123

CONFERENCE TECHNIQUE QUICK REFERENCE 126

PROFESSIONAL REFERENCES 128

Introduction

After two years of full-time study for an MFA in creative writing and literature, I debated if I should return to teaching. I had taught secondary-level English for nine years at that point, and I knew how difficult it was. For four glorious semesters, I had discussed poetry with peers and mentors who were as passionate as I about it. The thought of reentering the secondary classroom with an overloaded schedule, overloaded classes, and a less-than-enthusiastic audience wasn't exactly appealing. And yet, I loved teaching; I loved that moment when a single student "gets it," or writes something genuine and meaningful for the first time, or realizes his error in thinking fiction is boring or poetry is for snobs. I vacillated, but regardless of my inner struggle, I needed a job, and teaching secondary English was where my credentials mounted. I began to send out resumes.

Within a few weeks, I got a call from the Braintree Schools outside of Boston, regarding an opening in the English department at the high school; I resolutely went to the interview. After I sat down, Ann Keenan, the director of the English department, said, "I'm afraid I've brought you in here under false pretenses, Marilyn. Last week, our eighth-grade writing workshop teacher left, and I put your resume aside . . ." She described the class as a genuine workshop where I would guide the students in their writing by teaching mini-lessons and working with them individually. It was visionary; I didn't think things like this could happen in the public schools. The thought of teaching students singly, having one-on-one conversations, being able to take the time to connect with each one without losing all of the others sounded sublime. I shivered.

Ideally I would be able to teach writing the way I had always wanted to in my overloaded classrooms, but didn't think I could. I quickly realized that instead of spending all my time and energy "teaching" writing prompts, I could have led a writing workshop and achieved better results. In a workshop, the students are more motivated and invested in their writing. They are more connected, both to their topics and to me. Additionally, I can constantly evolve as a writing teacher: I can tinker with the assignments themselves, tweaking them each year; I can vary the advice I give each student and note the result.

I have also learned that the intensity of a workshop can be exhausting. It requires constant and genuine thought as well as attention. It requires familiarity with a wealth of sources—all of my training, experience, and reading—to make it through any given day. I have about 100 students, divided into five classes. By the end of the day I am often "conferenced out." Helping students write about their experiences, feelings, and beliefs while fielding their questions, concerns, ambivalence, impatience, frustration, and inattentiveness constantly challenges me.

But the results are worth the work: Every single student improves as a writer over the year. I don't think I could have ever said that in my previous teaching positions. And what's more, I get to know the students. I get to know their gifts, their families, their losses. I get to know their loves and their fears. I get to show just the right poem to a girl writing about her grandfather's empty chair. I learn that one boy who scowls during most mini-lessons loves auto races, and attends them with his father. I learn that one girl who can barely make eye contact with anyone is an award-winning gymnast. I get to praise them specifically and genuinely. I get to question them pointedly and personally, pushing them to look deeper within themselves. It is, simply put, a gift.

I realize that very few schools have whole classes set aside for writing workshop, and that English teachers are expected to instruct students in reading, literature, writing, and grammar in their allotted time; I was there. Creating time for a writing workshop segment of class may seem impossible, but I have learned that nothing works as effectively as an in-class workshop with one-on-one teacher-student discussions—not writing at home, not responding to prompts in class. Students need class time to think and be guided in their writing. Of course, as English teachers, we know that writing makes people better human beings. But there are more practical reasons to justify the time, such as standardized testing, college entrance tests, and college application essays, to name a few. We must use these pressures to demand in-class writing time if we do not have it already.

This book is for anyone who has ever carved out, fought for, stolen, or simply been given the time to meet with students one-on-one to discuss what they are writing. I hope that the information, techniques, and stories presented here will ease the exhausting part of the job and help teachers effectively guide their students to create genuine, meaningful pieces. When this happens, all parties learn more about each other, themselves, and the world. This is the rich reward of writing.

ABOUT THE BOOK

- The conversations presented here are collected from memories of conversations I have had with various students. I have used all of these techniques numerous times.

- The reader will notice that the students represented in the book range from submissive to enthusiastic, and from below average to extremely bright, but all of them are cooperative. I have used only these success stories because I handle any disrespectful behavior, including the outright refusal to write, with a series of disciplinary measures that do not need to be outlined here.

- For the most part, the chapters are arranged in a sequential order that mirrors the building of a piece of writing. However, many topics overlap, and in an actual conference, one topic will crop up in the middle of discussing another. I have not edited that reality out of this book, so the reader will find departures, such as a brief exchange about introductions, for example, in the chapter about organization, even though the chapter on introductions comes later.

- Likewise, instead of devoting an entire chapter to grammar, I have included discussions of grammar within conversations on other elements, which is how they occur in real life.

- Finally, in the back of the book is a quick reference of techniques encompassing the ideas illustrated in the conversations presented here.

CHAPTER 1

Behind the Scenes of a Conference

Productive conferences—ones that lead to meaningful, polished pieces of writing—happen within a well-organized, smooth-running, predictable workshop setting in which students actively participate without disturbing others. This is no small task. But many questions that could arise in a conference and many problems that may occur when a teacher is trying to conference can be avoided if time and effort are first spent training the students in proper workshop routine and behavior. As is true outside the classroom, preventing problems before they start is easier than solving them later on. Like all teachers, I have learned and continue to learn through experience what problems I can eliminate with better preparation or better organization. In my first book, *Teaching Students to Write Effective Essays*, I discuss more fully how to set up and run a writing workshop. Here, I will give a briefer version.

Classroom Organization

The room should be organized so that all necessary materials are easily accessible to the students. Few situations frustrate me more than approaching a student's desk hoping to talk about the theme of her autobiographical essay and learning that she's been doodling for the past 20 minutes because she "can't find the dictionary." Having a well-organized room and familiarizing the students with the locations of items will eliminate many of these lame excuses. Students should have no problems or inhibitions helping themselves to pens, pencils, highlighters, paper, scissors, tape, dictionaries, thesauri, and grammar handbooks, as well as the writing assignments themselves and any applicable reading for each assignment.

Posters hung around the room have also proven quite handy during conferencing. Most of mine are homemade. During a conference, I can refer to one in conversation, point to one nearby, or send the student across the room to examine one closely. I also post lists generated during mini-lessons around the room.

EASY-TO-ACCESS MATERIALS

- ☐ Assignment sheets
- ☐ Sample reading
- ☐ Blank paper
- ☐ Editing/revising check sheets
- ☐ Pens, pencils, highlighters
- ☐ Dictionaries and thesauri
- ☐ Stapler
- ☐ Scissors and tape

POSTERS

- ☐ Transition Words (different colors for different kinds)
- ☐ Words Used in a Two-Part Sentence*
- ☐ Commonly Confused Homophones
- ☐ Homophones of Contractions
- ☐ Banned Words
- ☐ Words Instead of "Said"
- ☐ Ways to Change Linking Verbs

* *a complex sentence; these are introductory words for dependent clauses*

Workshop Procedure

The workshop must be able to run without conspicuous leadership. The students should know what their work is and be familiar enough with the writing process that they can work on their own for days at a time. Of course, they won't be working totally on their own, but they should feel largely independent. I use step-by-step assignment sheets that walk students through the writing process for each piece. For each assignment, students must read models, answer questions about the reading, prewrite, draft, revise, and edit. When a student completes one assignment, he can go to the Assignment Crate, where all assignments and reading are filed, and obtain the subsequent assignment. This ensures that each student always has work to do, regardless of his or her individual pace. Having work to do and knowing how to do it eliminates constant questioning. I strive to create an atmosphere where each student knows that once we begin a conference, we most likely won't be disturbed.

> **TIP**
>
> On the Assignment Sheets, use empty check boxes ☐ as bullets for each step, so that students can check off each completed task. Keep tasks small and specific, such as "Organize your brainstorm into groups of ideas."

Silence

At any stage of the writing process, if students are working hard, they should be silent. The only exception would be a very low-voiced peer reading. I feel that the potential distractions caused by peer reading outweigh the benefits, but I know of other teachers who believe that much is gained from it. At any rate, everyone else should be quietly working. Students must know that my focusing on one student does not mean everyone else can talk.

Topics for Writing

In her book *In the Middle* (1998), Nancie Atwell explains how she helps students generate a list of topics in the beginning of the year. This technique, which she calls "writing territories" and I call "Topics for Writing," has proved invaluable to me. To cull as many ideas as possible from the students, I developed a questionnaire that I read aloud to the class as they write their lists. When I conduct this exercise on the first day of class, the lists often reach two or more pages in length. The students list the details of their lives: people, places, hobbies, favorites, fears, and moments. Most students are eager to brainstorm in this way because motivation is high at the beginning of the year and because listing is easy. (Delving into the topic is more difficult, but they don't know that yet.) They keep these lists all year and can refer to them for any assignment. Since I implemented this ritual, rarely does a student tell me that she has nothing to write. And when this does happen, at least we have a place to start looking.

SOME "TOPICS FOR WRITING" QUESTIONS

- *What is your favorite season? Why?*
- *Write about a time when you were afraid.*
- *What makes you angry?*
- *What are you good at?*
- *Describe one of your favorite belongings.*

Mini-lessons

Mini-lessons can be used for a number of purposes: to brainstorm, to address particular difficulties with certain assignments, to explain grammar, and to give tips on technique, to name a few. The mini-lesson can teach something that would otherwise have to be explained in a dozen individual conferences. If while conferencing I notice a recurring problem students are having that I didn't anticipate, I can address the problem in a mini-lesson. Different classes may require different mini-lessons. Students take notes on every mini-lesson in their writing notebooks, which never leave the room. That way, they have a personal writing handbook available to them in class. I often refer students to these during conferences.

> **TIP**
>
> *Set a minimum length for each assignment. I require every essay to be at least one typed page (Times New Roman, 12 pt, double-spaced with 1" margins). Since this is a house rule, students know they must push themselves in order to get full points on the grading rubric.*

However a writing workshop is set up, preparation, routine, and discipline make it work. I take several days at the start of each year to train students to follow the procedures I have chosen, and I post signs around the class to serve as reminders to help them maintain order and silence.

CHAPTER 2

General Conference Guidelines

No two conferences or workshops ever flow exactly the same way. Still, there are patterns to how often I conference, where, and for how long, as well as a consistency to the content.

Frequency

Generally, I aim to visit every student every class. This happens about two-thirds of the time for me, depending greatly on class size, the level of the class (my students are grouped homogeneously), and the assignment itself. Some assignments are more difficult, and students need much guidance. For example, although I give thorough mini-lessons leading up to an assignment called "Analysis of a Poem," most students need help unlocking the language of their chosen poems, and much conference time is spent doing just that. Consequently, I can only get to seven or eight students in one 50-minute class.

I do not have a set order in which I visit students. Sometimes I simply scan the room and start with the student who looks most confused, frustrated, bored, or distracted. Other times I take the stack of corrected assignments waiting to be revised and conference with students as I return their papers. If a student has major revisions to make, I will try to gauge if it is wise to disturb her from what she is writing. If she is deep within her writing, I might just lean over and tell her that I have work for her to revise, and she should raise her hand or come to my desk when she is ready to revise it. On the other hand, if a student looks stuck, he usually welcomes the chance to revise a previous assignment and give his mind a rest from the current one.

Returning papers aside, if a student is clearly engrossed in writing, I rarely disturb him. I know myself how difficult it can be to get into the zone, and I have all the comforts of home around me when I write. So even after I've conferenced with everyone else, if the remaining student is writing intently, I'll wait until the next day and try to meet her first before she reenters the piece. If I miss a student one day, I try not let another class pass without a conference.

At any point between my conferences with various students, a student can raise his hand and I will go to him immediately. Often the question is short, but it can serve as a springboard for a longer conference if needed. Sometimes, after I see all the students for that day, I sit at my desk for the final minutes of class and begin the day's grading. Students often approach me with questions at this time, or with revisions based on an earlier conference. Although I cannot do this during every class, I find this practice fruitful; often students can't organize their thoughts on the spot when I appear at their desks for a regular conference, but given time, they can formulate intelligent questions and approach me at their own pace. I always keep an extra chair at my desk.

I neither keep track of how often I meet with each student nor record the content of my conferences. In the beginning I did, but I found these rituals to be tedious and distracting. Even with some classes of 22 or more, I can remember whom I've seen recently and who needs a visit. I know that I conference with every student multiple times over any given assignment. Certainly, keeping track could benefit a teacher during meetings with parents or administration and I do not discourage it; for me, though, I find it unnecessary. I have never needed such records either in or out of the classroom; the drafts, and my notes on them, speak for themselves.

> **TIP**
>
> *In addition to visiting students in some orderly way, plan for free time at your desk so students can approach you at their own pace.*

Location

I do not have a set conference area. In my room at any given moment, some students are at their desks, some are at their computers (which line the perimeter of the room), some are at the bookshelves getting materials, one or two may be at my desk organizing a finished paper to be handed in, and another one is at the filing cabinet storing a revised, graded assignment. I usually find a space near the student I want to see, grabbing a computer chair or wedging myself into a nearby desk. I don't like to lean over the student for a conference; I prefer to be at eye level, so I seem more like a collaborator than an authority figure. Also, leaning down gives the impression that I want to keep moving, and I like the student to feel like my total attention is with him. I also don't like to squat at the student's desk. It puts me lower than the student, and can get uncomfortable, both of which can distract the student from the work at hand. If there is no room in the immediate vicinity of the student, I invite her to my desk.

Wherever we are, I want the student to feel that she has my full attention and that at that moment, nothing is more important to me than the success of the piece and her own growth as a writer and thinker.

> **TIP**
>
> *Sit at eye level with the student, not higher or lower.*

Duration

I try to keep the conferences short—five minutes or less—in order to keep the student moving. Nothing kills writing momentum more than talking to the teacher for half the class. Also, shorter conferences keep the rest of the students focused, and I have more opportunities to circulate and monitor. That said, when it feels appropriate and the student remains engaged, some conferences do run longer than five minutes.

Often, as will be demonstrated in subsequent chapters, I break up a conference into two sessions or more. For example, I will give the student some concrete task, such as making a specific list or underlining all the verbs,

> **TIP**
>
> *Try multiconferencing. Instead of conducting one long conference with a student, give a small task, conference with two or three other students, and then check on the progress of the original student, assigning another small task if necessary and repeating the process.*

and leave that student to conference with another. I check back when I sense the task is completed and direct the student to the next step. This technique of multiconferencing keeps the students thinking and allows me to visit as many students as possible. Completing bite-size tasks is an especially effective means of building the confidence of students who are stuck or struggling.

Content

During a conference, I will talk about anything at all that will help further the success of a piece of writing. At any given moment, I act as detective, coach, instructor, psychiatrist, audience, archaeologist, cheerleader, or disciplinarian. I play these roles throughout the book, but the two main pillars that support each conference are the use of praise and the focus on meaning.

Praise

I always begin a conference with a positive comment. Sometimes this is easy; sometimes I have to search. I cannot fake it though, not only because adolescents sense duplicity and loathe it, but more important, because I want to genuinely encourage them. So I search. I'm not afraid to be silent at first, either reading what they have written or shuffling through drafts and notes. The students are used to watching me think in front of them. And without fail, something, somewhere, exists for me to praise. Even in the worst-case scenario, when a student is angrily sitting in front of a single blank sheet of paper in total defiance, I can say something like "You wrote a wonderful ode a couple of weeks ago; you're good at describing. I know you are perfectly capable of doing this assignment as well." I don't mean coddling—students must always know that they are expected to work hard and thoughtfully—but honest, appropriate praise can often go a long way toward rejuvenating a stuck student, perking up a lazy student, or reengaging a distracted student who is on the verge of misbehaving. With most papers, I can easily find something—a rich prewrite, a well-written intro, an original simile, well-organized paragraphs, *something*—that merits sincere appreciation. And if many aspects of the work warrant note, I take the time to do it. In addition to allowing me to connect with the student, praise engages the student even further into the writing: When he knows that parts of the piece succeed, he is motivated to revise those that lag.

TIP

Address students by name during every conference. This simple technique does much to make the student feel connected and valued.

I always avoid talking about talent. Even if a student is wildly talented and so naturally gifted that there is little I can teach him, I refrain from saying, "Wow, you're so gifted" or "You have so much talent" or "You should think about becoming a professional writer." I will, on occasion, tell a student who is struggling with a certain aspect of her writing the she is a "natural" at one technique or another, in order to boost her confidence, but that kind of praise is extremely specific and clearly used to lift spirits. I would never make a sweeping comment about any student's overall ability, good or bad, during a writing conference. The main reason is that it would discourage the other students in the class. In addition, it may embarrass the student. If anything, I might tell a student how talented I thought she was in a private conference at the end of the year, or, if appropriate, during a private parent conference during the year.

Meaning Before Grammar

When looking at a piece for the first time, I check to see if it's substantial enough to deal with as a draft. If not, I must help the student build it up from the inside out. If the draft seems sufficient, then I generally direct student revision from outside in: first organization, then details, examples, and language, and then grammar. I resist the urge to fix (or have the student fix) all the little grammar mistakes as I read. At first, this was like stepping on small stones in a yard: somewhat painful and definitely annoying, but I learned to let it go. It is a waste of energy to address all conventions early on in a piece, unless the muddled grammar obscures the meaning to the point of confusion. Often, the student will correct something on her own in the middle of the conference; this is natural. But for me to dive into the grammatical issues of a piece at the beginning of a conference dampens the student's momentum and enthusiasm. A writer writes in order to say something meaningful, and if I bypass the meaning in favor of perfecting the grammar, the student is apt to feel discouraged and even slighted.

That said, I do not wait until the final conference to talk about grammar. Often it will come up once the process of revising the details, organization, tone, and such is underway. As the following conversations show, once I have a student confidently revising one aspect of the draft, I will mention a pattern of grammatical mistakes that needs attention. Although meaning trumps grammar in the initial conferences, grammar is not insignificant; it is merely secondary. Also, the number of grammar mistakes plays a role: If a student has mangled every mark of punctuation, after our conferences over other aspects of the piece I do a full lesson on punctuation. If a student missed one apostrophe, I wait until the student hands the paper in to circle the spot and let him figure it out on his own. And if, say, a mild pattern of switching verb tense appears in the paper, I will mention it amid other revisions, as described above.

If a student's paper is saturated with every imaginable grammatical error, I would first help her develop the major aspects of the piece, such as the details, theme, and organization—usually, these areas will need major improvements as well—and then choose only one or two grammatical topics to focus on for an entire class, or longer if needed. In the following assignment, I would move to the next point in grammar.

Overall, I enjoy helping students master the conventions of our language. It empowers them. With grammar, I try to take the tone of a teammate rather than a teacher, acknowledging when the rules of grammar are difficult or even illogical, while communicating my belief in the student's ability to grasp them.

Regardless of the topic, during each conference my underlying purpose is to convey confidence. I expect and assume that students are trying their best. My ultimate goal is always to help them improve from where they are. They will not all end up as great writers, nor will they be mini-versions of myself. But I believe that all of them can grow as a writers and thinkers, and that their lives will be richer for it. It is with this conviction that I approach the students to discuss what parts of their minds, hearts, and lives they have put on paper for me to read.

CHAPTER 3

"I Don't Have Anything to Write"

I know better than to take this comment personally, but when I hear a student say "I don't have anything to write," it always feels like a punch in the stomach. I think to myself, "Isn't the assignment interesting enough? Weren't my mini-lessons engaging? Isn't the model reading inspiring enough for you?" Part of the discomfort comes from knowing how much effort it can take to pull a topic out of an unwilling participant. Sometimes, the issue can resolve itself quickly, especially if a list of Topics for Writing exist.

As mentioned in the first chapter, for each writing assignment in my class, students work from a detailed Assignment Sheet that outlines the steps they should take to complete the piece. Students must first read at least two sample pieces—two finished essays, stories, poems, and so on—before they start to write. They then answer four or five questions for each example. These questions check for comprehension as well as direct students' attention to certain technical aspects of the piece, and I factor their answers into the overall grade for the assignment.

AUTOBIOGRAPHY

Brainstorming for Topics

In the scenario below, the students are working on autobiographical essays about some past experience that stands out in their minds. As I circulate around the room, I see Dan elaborately decorating the corner of the Autobiography Assignment Sheet.

Ms. P: How's it going, Dan?

Dan: I don't have anything to write about.

Ms. P: Sometimes that happens. Did you do the reading?

Dan: Yeah.

Ms. P: *(I look over his answers to the reading questions.)* Okay, it looks like you did do the reading and understood it well. Good job so far. *(I found something to praise.)* What did you

> *I always ask; I never take it for granted that the student has actually read the sample essays given with the assignment. If Dan hasn't done the reading, I'll tell him he must do it before we can proceed.*

think of the author's decision at the end, to go with her dad to put down the dog? *(I'm trying to engage him.)*

Dan: I don't know. It was good.

Ms. P: I thought she was brave. I don't think I could ever do something like that. *(Still trying.)*

Dan: Me neither.

Ms. P: Do you have a dog?

Dan: Yeah.

Ms. P: What kind?

Dan: A yellow Lab. She's three.

Ms. P: Did she ever get lost, like the dog in the story?

Dan: No. One time she was outside for a while and came back with scratches on her nose, but she was all right. We never knew what happened.

Ms. P: That might make an interesting poem someday: imagining what happened to her out there. You should add that to your Topics for Writing if you don't have it there already. Take a second to write it down. *(He does.)* Did you try any prewriting after you did the reading?

> *Besides trying to connect with Dan, I'm trying to demonstrate that ideas for writing are just regular ideas and events that we look closely at. They are swirling around in our everyday conversations and thoughts; we need only to pluck them from memory and examine them more deeply.*

Dan: No. I can't think of anything.

Ms. P: Let's take a look at the rest of your Topics for Writing while you have it open. Do you mind if I look at it with you?

Dan: No.

> *I ask this because at the beginning of the year when I guide the students in creating their Topics for Writing lists, I tell them that they need not worry about being graded or critiqued on the content; the list is for their reference only.*

> *Often, a student will find a topic in this list when we read it through together. Or I might see an interesting entry that I can inquire about. Sometimes the list is scant or the student doesn't like what's there for this particular assignment. Dan's list doesn't have much on it.*

Ms. P: What does this one mean: "Jack in fifth grade?"

Dan: That was just a friend I had back then.

Ms. P: Can you think of a time with him to write about?

Dan: Not really. I mean, I just don't know.

Ms. P: Are you sure? Nothing funny that happened? Or scary? What was he like?

Dan: He was always joking around and getting in trouble. I don't think I want to write about him. I just don't know what to pick. My life is pretty boring. There's nothing unusual about it.

> *This is a common belief among students, and I spend the year trying to dispel it.*

Ms. P: There doesn't have to be, Dan! Believe me, anybody's life is interesting if you look closely enough at it. That's what writers do: They examine life and find small details other people overlook. I guarantee that you have something interesting to write about because if you're alive at all, if you have a life, there's going to be events and people and places in it that are interesting. It's not about the actual events anyway—it's about how you tell about them, how closely you look at them. Does that make sense?

Dan: Sort of.

Ms. P: Well, look at the girl in the reading. Her dog died. How many dogs do you think die each day around the world?

Dan: I don't know. Hundreds?

Ms. P: At least. It's sad, but it happens all over. So what makes her story interesting?

Dan: The way she tells it, I guess?

Ms. P: Yes! She tells it so you feel like you are there. Let's look at the last paragraph. Read it one more time, right now, and underline any details that jump out at you. Think of your five senses—sight, sound, taste, smell, and touch. Go ahead. *(I point to the last paragraph on the sample reading. He reads.)*

Dan: Okay.

Ms. P: Good. What did you notice?

Dan: She just describes it really well.

Ms. P: Read the parts you underlined. *(I always direct students to the actual text.)*

Dan: "His eyes seemed to empty as he looked at me" . . . "The soft fur on his belly stilled as I stroked it." Parts like that.

Ms. P: Good. Those are sight details, aren't they? And a touch detail—stroking the fur. You feel what she feels. She makes you care about her and her dog just for a few minutes. See? It's not about having some crazy life; it's about looking closely at the life you have. Do you understand?

Dan: I guess.

Ms. P: Okay. I definitely want to see you do well on this assignment, Dan, and I think you can. What I want you to do right now, off the top of your head, is to make some short lists for me. I want you to think of three times each when something funny, scary, or sad happened in your life. *(I write "Funny," "Scary," and "Sad" at the top of a blank piece of paper.)* Anything. Also, think of one time you did something brave, like the girl in the reading. It can be small. *(I write "Brave.")* I'll check back in a couple minutes. Just jot down a couple phrases in each category. Then we'll look at them together. Can you try that? Don't worry if it's "good" or not; just make the lists and we will worry about what we can use later. Will you try?

> *Many times laziness can lead to the feeling of being overwhelmed that comes with the statement of "I don't have anything to write." Gently reminding a student that he will be graded on his work (or lack thereof) might help get the creative juices flowing.*

Dan: Okay.

While circulating around the room conferencing with other students, I occasionally glance at Dan to make sure he is writing and not daydreaming. After some minutes, I return.

> *I'm trying to break up the task and minimize it. Sometimes the thought of selecting one topic from an entire life blocks the student. Hopefully, focusing on small chunks will feel more manageable to Dan.*

Ms. P: So, what have you got? *(I look at his lists.)* Good, you came up with a few ideas for each category. This is a great start. *(Praise.)*

Dan: Yeah, but I could only think of one thing for "Scary."

Ms. P: That's alright. You have plenty of other good ideas to work with here. Now, which one seems most interesting to you? *(I resist choosing the one that seems most interesting to me.)*

Dan: Maybe . . . the time we went to Disney World. *(Not the one I would have chosen.)*

Ms. P: Okay. What about it stands out for you? Why did you write it down?

Dan: Well, I went there with my dad and mom and brother, and we went on this one ride, Space Mountain, and it was funny. *(I'm hoping there's more to this.)*

Ms. P: When did you go?

Dan: Last January.

Ms. P: In the middle of school?

Dan: Yeah. It was the only time my dad could get off, since he travels so much, and he promised we would take a trip together as a family.

Ms. P: You must have been happy when he told you you would go.

Dan: We were. He came home from work one night and gave us a wrapped box. The tickets were inside. *(Hold everything! That's something we can use.)*

Ms. P: Really? How exciting! Do you think that would be a good place to start, on that night when he came home with the mysterious wrapped box?

Dan: Maybe. Even my mom was surprised. My brother and I ripped it open together.

Ms. P: Let's try it. Make a list of anything you remember from that night, anything at all: what you were doing when your dad came home, what color the wrapping paper was, what your mom said when she realized what it was. Think of your five senses again and write anything that comes to mind. Think of as much as you can, and don't worry if you can't remember something perfectly—just write what you can remember. Don't worry if the details seem too small— write everything and you can cut what you don't want later. *(I write some more categories on his paper: "Sights," "Colors," "Sounds," "Quotes," and "Feelings.")*

Dan: Okay. It was leftover Christmas wrapping paper. And it was a bigger box with a lot of tissue paper and the tickets at the bottom. *(He senses my excitement and is encouraged.)*

Ms. P: That's great! Write it down. *(He does.)* Keep going, and I'll check back. Just write anything you can possibly remember, Dan. I think this will be a wonderful essay.

When helping a student choose a topic, I strive to identify something the student cares about, and find the heart of it. If the student has no emotional investment in the topic, the writing will not succeed. It is my job to open the dialogue, to get the students to talk about their lives. I have found that most students will talk about the people, objects, places, events, and ideas that are meaningful to them when asked. Leading them to the core of the matter, where the theme resides, is more challenging. Often I see a glimmer of what it might be when the student first starts describing the potential subject, but I must remind myself not to put thoughts or words into a student's pen. Over a series of conferences I will let the topic unfold while simultaneously pushing the student to dig deeper until we have arrived at the crux, clear and sparkling under the layers of description and plot.

VARIATION

I would choose different categories to brainstorm depending on the genre of the assignment. For example, if this were a persuasive essay, I would ask the student what makes her angry or at least irritated, either at home, in school, outside of school, in her town, or in the world. I would write "Home," "School," "Town" and "World" as brainstorming topic headings on her paper. For an ode, I would ask the student to list his favorite people, places, and belongings. For a compare-and-contrast essay, I would have the students think of hobbies, things they know well, and people and places they're familiar with. The idea is to give the student small, concrete, attainable steps.

My hope is that he will generate enough from the initial incident to complete an essay without even having to extend it to the actual trip to Florida—although the memory of the ride at Disney World might serve as an effective and symbolic concluding image, depending on how the essay shapes up. In future conferences, I will help Dan plumb this moment even more; I will ask him about daily life in his house with his father traveling and what his dad means to him.

CHAPTER 4

Only Bones: Generating Details

Unlike Dan, many students can think of a topic without hesitation, but often they either write a half page of bare-boned facts and announce, "I have nothing else to write," or, knowing that one typed page is required, they extend the topic to include any lifeless generality that peripherally relates to the original idea. Either way, the problem is the same: no detail. No looking closely. No deeper thought.

It's hard not to wince at the prospect of a conference on a one-page story about a two-week stint at hockey camp. With these kinds of pieces, I do my best to identify anything unusual, anything with a hint of feeling, to start with. I try to whittle the writing down to the original topic or if there was none to begin with, I find a small section of the piece to focus on. The conversation runs much like the one in the previous chapter, as I question the student about her life, looking for a moment that holds some promise for a short essay.

If the piece is too short, I start with what is there and try to mine as many details as possible. In *Teaching Students to Write Effective Essays*, I describe a mini-lesson that leads the class through an exercise in developing sensory details. Although the mini-lesson usually convinces students that sensory details improve a piece of writing, often they must be individually pushed to conjure details and include them in their own essays.

AUTOBIOGRAPHY

Using the Five Senses, Taking Notes in the Field

In the following example, the student has a topic for his autobiographical essay, but has no idea how he is going to fill a page. It will take several conferences to shape this piece to completion. It needs a theme, an introduction, a new title, and of course, many more details. That is where we begin.

> *Early that morning my uncle called me on the phone and told me that he was going to bring some magazine's for my birthday. Around twelve I was eating my birthday cake and I herd a sound and the sound sounded like a lawn mower getting started. I did not pay attention to it and my friend came running to the door and yelled "There is a go-cart outside and it is with your uncle."*

I did not believe him so I went outside and saw it and I was speechless. My family yelled, "Happy Birthday!" That by far was the best birthday gift.

Ms. P: Okay, Steve, you have a good idea here for an essay. That's a pretty nice gift, isn't it? You must have been thrilled.

Steve: I was. I couldn't believe it.

Ms. P: Tell me about the go-cart.

Steve: It's dark green and goes really fast.

Ms. P: The doors and hood are dark green?

Steve: No, it's made of bars mostly. It doesn't have doors.

Ms. P: Oh, so it's mostly open! You're going to be the expert on this one, Steve—I have to confess I don't know a thing about go-carts. You're going to be teaching me here. Okay, so it's just bars and open space.

Steve: Yeah, when you're riding it, it's really loud and windy.

Ms. P: Right—you used a vivid simile in your description of the sound—"like a lawnmower getting started." Good one.

Steve: Thanks.

Ms. P: What I want you to do now is think of more details like that. Think of your five senses. Remember what they are? *(Sometimes they don't!)*

Steve: Yeah, um, seeing, hearing, smelling, touching, and . . . tasting.

Ms. P: Right. Now imagine that you are riding in the go-cart. What else do you hear? What do you feel? What do you smell? What do you see? If it's possible, do you taste anything? Think back to the first time you rode it and ask yourself these questions. Jot down anything, anything at all that comes to mind. *(As I'm talking, I write down categories: "Sounds," "Feelings," "Smells," "Sights," and "Tastes.")* By "feelings" I mean what you physically felt on your body, but you can also put any emotions you felt too. Let's start with what you just told me. You said the go-cart is made of dark green bars. Where would that go?

Steve: Under "Sights."

Ms. P: Good. Write it there. *(He does.)* How about "like a lawnmower"? Where would that go?

Steve: Under "Sounds."

Ms. P: Exactly. You've got the idea. Can you remember more details like these, do you think?

Steve: Definitely.

Ms. P: Good. I'll check back.

When I stop back at Steve's desk, his lists look like this:

> *I want to bring his emotional connection to the go-cart to the surface and proceed from there.*

> *Whenever I can, I tell students when they know more than I do on a subject. I spend so much time and energy instructing them, directing them, guiding them; I want them to remember that they, as writers, are also educating me. This builds confidence and sends the message that even at their age, they have lived long enough to know some things well.*

> *I underline the simile. I always use literary terms whenever I can, as if they are a normal part of everyday conversation. However, I also phrase them in a way so that the student knows what I'm talking about and doesn't feel "dumb."*

Sounds	Feelings	Smells	Sights	Tastes
like a lawnmower	like flying	gas	dark green bars	birthday cake
like a chainsaw	wind on my cheeks	???	blur of trees	exhaust in the
silence, then wheels	pressing the gas		new cars	beginning
peeling out	pedal		new streets	
	bumpy, hitting			
	my head			
	happy			

Even though I find details such as "like flying," "happy," and "birthday cake" general and bland, I don't say anything. Instead, I will press him with questions I know he can answer. Telling him "'Happy' is such an obvious answer. Try to think of some other feelings" would discourage him and probably cause him to shut down. Since it's early in the year, I let a few generalities remain in the piece as a trade-off for the long-term gains to Steve's confidence and interest in writing. Throughout the year, little by little, I will push him to think more specifically and phase out the weaker details from his writing.

Ms. P: Okay, Steve, it looks like you have some interesting and specific details here. And you have some more similes—excellent. *(I star the similes as I'm talking.)* I also especially like "blur of trees." What do "new cars" and "new streets" mean?

Steve: Well, I was so close to them, they seemed new, like I had never noticed them before.

Ms. P: Excellent. Look at them again in your mind. Think of what colors they were. *(I write "Colors?" in the margin next to "Sights.")* Think of what else was on the streets. Name those things exactly. *(I write "Other things?" next to "new streets.")*

Steve: Okay.

Ms. P: The other thing I want you to remember is the weather that day. Think of how it felt—was it hot, cool, humid? Think of the light—was it cloudy, bright, overcast, or something else? *(I write "Weather" in an open space.)* Write down whatever you remember or think you remember. I'll be back in a couple minutes.

> Often, kids are reluctant to write down something if they're not 100 percent sure of it. I always tell them to trust their memories; even if they aren't completely sure of a detail, they can describe what they think it might have been. Philosophical and ethical debates about "truth" in memoir aside, it is just an easy way to get ideas flowing.

When I check back a second time, he has added more details:

Sounds	Feelings	Smells	Sights-Colors?	Tastes	Weather/Light
like a lawnmower	like flying	gas	dark green bars	birthday cake	humid
like a chainsaw	wind on my cheeks	???	blur of trees	exhaust in the	summertime
silence, then wheels	pressing the		new cars-blue,	beginning	breeze
peeling out	gas pedal		green, red,		blue sky
	bumpy, hitting		like a tunnel		bright
	my head		new streets—		
	happy		**Other things?**		
			up close, yellow lines,		
			gravel, flowers		

Ms. P: Excellent work, Steve! We've got plenty here to start with. Now, always feel free to add anything else that pops into your head as you're writing. That's how most writers write: as they're writing, new ideas come up and they jot them down. Do the same when that happens to you.

Steve: Okay.

Ms. P: Good. Now, I want you to go back to your story, and start adding some of these. Check them off as you do, so you know which ones you used. Work on that for the rest of class. Start by checking off the ones that are already in there right now.

Steve: Okay. *(He does.)*

Ms. P: Also, you have an assignment for tonight: I want you to take a notepad and a pen, go in your garage, and sit in the go-cart. Spend some time there. Note down anything you notice: the feel of the seat, the shape of the wheel, the feeling of the bars around you, anything. Write down ten details—don't worry if they're "good" or "boring" or whatever; there are no wrong answers—just get to ten.

Steve: Ten? How can I think of another ten?

Ms. P: Don't worry; you will easily be able to do it when you're sitting in the go-cart. Right now it seems like a lot because you're not there. If you're allowed to take it out for a ride this afternoon, do that too, and write down ten additional details about that. This is how writers do research: they try to experience, or reexperience, the thing they're writing about, noticing every little detail about it. Can you do that?

Steve: I'll try it. Twenty details sounds like a lot though.

Ms. P: Here's a trick: *(My tone says that I'm letting him in on a secret that I shouldn't.)* For the sounds, use onomatopoeia—meaning, the sound is the word. For example, you did it already: "peeling out" sounds a bit like the tires making that high-pitched sound, doesn't it? Peeeeeeeeeling. *(My voice gets high.)* See?

Steve: Yeah.

Ms. P: Now, you thought of that one without even trying, which means you're a natural at it. While you're driving, look for sounds, and try to think of the word that the sound actually is. For example, instead of "birds singing," write "chirping;" instead of "horns," write "honks." See how easy it is? Right now, think of another sound for the tires.

Steve: Um . . . "screech"?

Ms. P: Exactly! The sound is the word. That little technique will help you in the Sounds department; do your best on the rest as well. Just relax, sit, drive the go-cart, and pay attention. You'll get to twenty. *(I write "Onomatopoeia" next to his "Sounds" category.)*

I constantly try to show the students that they are using the same techniques "real" writers use, and that they are "real" writers themselves.

Again, I'm trying to drive home the idea that writers use the stuff of their lives to infuse details in their writing. I assigned Steve 20 details for the same reason I insist that each assignment be at least one typed page: the more writing, the better the chance of something good being written. Ideas beget ideas. Moreover, most students (and adults!) work well with tasks that provide a specific goal, an ending point; it takes out some of the "artsy" nebulousness of writing that so often confounds students and makes them think they can't write. They may not think they can write a descriptive paper, but a list of 20 details they can do.

TIP

Set a number of details for the student to summon.

Steve: Can you sign my homework sheet?

Steve is one of our homework-sheet kids, meaning that all of his teachers must initial his assignments each night for his parents. With delight, he writes "Sit in go-cart and drive it" under the "Writing Workshop" category. After adding "List 20 additional details" and "Driving only if allowed," I initial my approval.

Encouraging students to somehow relive the experience or a part of the experience or, in the case of fiction writing, to experience for the first time what they are writing about, is the most effective way to gather details. This "in the field" research requires the writer to not simply experience something firsthand, but also to take notes. The problem in a writing workshop is that it just isn't practical to send our students into the world in the middle of the day so they can retrace their steps to the corner store or the town lake, or even just stand outside and take notes on fresh air, fog, or snow. Parents don't always appreciate such homework assignments, and even if they do, that does not guarantee it will get done. The student must have the genuine enthusiasm for the subject that Steve does to want to rush home to do writing research. That said, I do try to inspire enthusiasm by making the real-life research part of the "Process" portion of the grade when I need to. Students are always welcome to use outside sources—the Internet, encyclopedias, books—to research details about places, climates, or certain objects, but in the end, students must do what other writers do: use their imaginations.

Steve proudly displays his findings the next day. On his paper, now a bit crumpled, he added the following:

Sounds Onomatopoeia	Feelings	Smells	Sights-Colors?	Tastes	Weather/Light

like a
   lawnmower
 	
like a chainsaw
 	
silence, then
   wheels peeling
   out
• scraping gravel
• people calling
• bumps
knocking
• roar
• swish of other
cars passing
• purr of engine
idling
• chirping
	like flying
	
	wind on
	   my cheeks
	
	pressing the
	   gas pedal
	
	bumpy—hitting
	   my head
	
	happy
	• leather-
	wrapped
	steering wheel
	• comfortable
	seat
	• like being
	in my
	own world—
	time capsule
	• exhilarating
	• sweating
		gas
		• grass
			dark green bars
			
			blur of trees
			
			new cars—blue,
			   green, red
			
			like a tunnel
			
			new streets
			
			Other things?
			up close, yellow
			   lines, gravel,
			   flowers
			• black gravel
			• neighbors
			turning to see
			• mailboxes
			• bars shinning
			• round steering
			wheel not a
			full circle
				birthday cake
				
				exhaust in the
				   beginning
				• sweat
					humid
					
					summertime
					
					breeze
					
					blue sky
					
					bright
					• afternoon sun

Ms. P: Wow! You did it! Excellent work! Was it fun?

Steve: Yeah. My mom wanted to see all 20 details when I was done.

Ms. P: That's great, Steve! What did she think of them?

Steve: She thought they were good.

Ms. P: Well, you'll have to be sure to bring home an extra copy of the final draft to show her.

Steve: Yeah.

Ms. P: Tell me about some of these—like "people calling." What does that mean?

Steve: When I was riding, one of my neighbors waved and called out to me. I couldn't really hear them, because the go-cart was so loud, but I put it as a sound anyway.

Ms. P: Good. Just jot down "waving" next to it so you have that extra information. How about "comfortable seat"? How exactly was it comfortable?

Steve: Well, a lot of times go-cart seats can be too small or too hard. This one is just right, though.

Ms. P: So, would you say "firm"?

Steve: Yeah, but comfortable.

Ms. P: Okay, so write down "firm but comfortable" in the margin next to that one. And "large" or "wide" or whatever you want to call it for the size. *(He writes "just right size." Inwardly cringing at the vague three bears reference, I let it go for now. I'll see what it looks like in the essay, if it makes it in.)* What is it made of?

> *I'm trying to push him but also help him along.*

Steve: Leather.

Ms. P: Good. Put that down too. Alright: first, you have to work these rich details into the story. *(I place his first draft next to the brainstorming list.)* Just start writing sentences using the details you have here. This is the easy part.

Steve: Okay . . . *(He doesn't believe me.)*

Ms. P: When we left off, you were standing outside, looking at the go-cart. Start there. What did you see? Use the details here, like "dark green bars" and "leather seat."

Steve: Oh! Okay. "It had dark green bars and a black leather seat."

Ms. P: Exactly! And do what you just did: add details if you think of them, like the color black.

Steve: Okay.

Ms. P: You can put more than one detail in a sentence. As I told you yesterday, you should check off the details as you use them. That way you can see what you've used and what's left. Let me know when you have a new draft and we'll go from there.

Steve: Okay.

Steve works for another class or two, adding in what he can. In passing, I remind him that he doesn't have to force in any details that don't seem to fit. When I next see the essay, it looks like this:

The Perfect Day

Early that morning my uncle called me on the phone and told me that he was going to bring some magazine's for my birthday. Around twelve I was eating my birthday cake and I herd a sound and the sound sounded like a lawn mower getting started. I did not pay attention to it and my friend came running to the door and yelled "There is a go-cart outside and it is with your uncle." I did not believe him so I went outside and saw it and I was speechless. My family yelled, "Happy Birthday!" That by far was the best birthday gift.

The go-cart had dark green bars and a black leather seat. It was a humid day in the summertime and I hoped in. I held on to the leather-wrapped steering wheel. I could smell the exhaust. I revved up the engine like a chainsaw and slowly backed up. My mom was clapping and jumping a little bit.

I backed into the street and for a second their was silence and birds chirping. And then I switched gears and stepped on the gas and broke that same silence. The wheels started to spin and it sounded like a car peeling out on a rocky driveway.

I was having a blast on my new go-cart. I was going as fast as I dreamed. I saw mailboxes and cars lined up on the street that I never noticed before. It was like going threw a tunnel. I was in a new world. Neighbors waved. The only down side of the day was the street I had been riding on was very bumpy and I was hitting my head every minute.

I came to a stop sign and stopped. I noticed the yellow lines on the street and black gravel. The purr of the engine was like a kitten.

I stepped on the gas and the wind was blowing on my cheeks. I was going so fast it felt like I was in the air flying away. I saw new streets I did not know were there. I felt like I was in my own world. It was like riding in a time capsule.

I got out of my go-cart and I was sweating. I went to my family and they smiled at me and then my dad said, "Your dream came true," and I smiled back. It was the best birthday ever.

I lavish praise on him when I read it; Steve has never written a full typed page of anything before and didn't think it possible. The next areas I will work on with Steve are theme, the introduction, and the conclusion. We have come this far, and even though "The Perfect Day" does not have to be perfect, it still needs these vital elements. For the introduction and conclusion, Steve can use some of the details he worked so hard to summon. Although identifying a theme will take a bit of new thought, Steve can again look to his list of details for help. A reward of carefully cultivating details is that one of them often points to a theme. The reason for this, I think, is the phenomenon of selective remembering: Out of all the myriad details alive in any moment, the ones we remember and choose to include in our writing are the ones that hold some meaning for us.

CHAPTER 5

Searching for Meaning: Cultivating Theme

Once a student has chosen a topic and brainstormed about it, either by listing, mapping, or freewriting, I always start to look for the theme. It does not (and often should not) have to be spelled out. Nor does it have to be clearly formed in the early stages of the essay, since a theme often reveals itself to a writer as he writes. The essay should, however, have a heartbeat. Without a glimmer of a theme, the piece has no meaning, no reason to exist, no justification to be read. The theme can change, deepen, or shift as the drafts evolve. It can start out as only a feeling, but the writer must have some sense of it, and must be willing to let it ripen. If students do not learn to write with the intention of having a theme, their pieces are dry bones, no matter how well crafted the description.

Any piece of writing can have a theme. It is up to the writer to discover it and convey it to the reader. Any topic a student chooses to write about comes from a multitude of possible topics in her consciousness—so obviously it has some meaning for her. I may be familiar with the topic, but I cannot assign it significance; only the writer of that particular piece can. My job is to ask her questions that will lead her to the deeper meaning of the piece.

I usually introduce theme early in the year, with the first autobiographical essay I assign. Students are usually comfortable writing an autobiography, and the genre serves as fertile ground for themes. To start, during a whole-class mini-lesson I give them short examples of stories with themes—maybe one page. Loren Eiseley's "The Green Gulch" is a useful model; it describes a child's first encounter with bullies, the herd mentality, and evil itself. Its theme is also clearly stated in the ending sentences.

Thinking in terms of theme may be difficult for students. Sure, they read short stories, novels, and plays and discuss themes such as growing up, survival, betrayal, and forgiveness, but to them, it can seem almost absurd to apply these ideas to their own lives. Even if they know an event is meaningful, they don't know how to, or don't want to, verbalize why. As a teacher, I cannot simply tell a student, "Take a few minutes and brainstorm some themes for this piece." Theme is something that already exists from the beginning, in the details, in the dialogue, in a comment that the

> Theme is not a moral. It's a view, a new twist on life through the writer's eyes.

student slipped in without plumbing the full meaning of it. My job, then, is to detect these rough nuggets when I see them, and to make a mental note (or even a written note) to return to them when the time is right in the progression of the piece. Then I can say to the writer, "Look what you wrote here. What does that mean? What is this really about?"

But even that is not enough. Never will a student answer, "Oh! That sentence reflects my fear of change. This essay is really about me coming of age!" Usually they play dumb, or even become reluctant or cranky. I have to keep pushing.

Sometimes I say to students who are in total denial, "Look, you wrote this piece. You remembered this event. Out of all the thousands or even millions of memories in your head, you chose this one. You chose all the details; you chose everything about it. It means something to you. It stands out for you. Your job as a writer is to figure out why." I want not only to get the student thinking, but also to suggest that she, the writer, controls the material.

I suggest to students what I think the piece really seems to be about. I may give more than one choice if I see the possibilities. Students appreciate this: Even if they feel they are being forced to think about theme, at least they can choose what kind of theme it's going to be. I try not to dictate any themes for them, but instead suggest themes to which the piece seems to lend itself. One easy way of finding a theme, I tell students, is to ask yourself what you learned from the experience. The student can simply begin a sentence with a phrase like, "I learned," "I realized," or "I knew then." With fiction, the writer must ask this question of her main character.

> With any genre, the reader asks the question: Why should I care?
>
>
>
> The answer to this question reveals the essay's theme.

Theme need not only apply to storytelling; a topic's importance and relevance can be communicated in other genres as well. In a persuasive essay, it's the reason readers should care about the writer's position, or how that position enriches their lives or life in general. In a compare-and-contrast essay, it's the meaning in the differences, or even the pleasure, the mindfulness, in noticing and analyzing the differences. Maybe the writer expresses a preference for one subject over the other in the compare-and-contrast piece. The essay then becomes persuasive, and meaning can be found there. A book review or short-story analysis that evaluates the story's themes and their significance illuminates an essay's own themes. All essays can have that deeper meaning that connects the reader to the topic and its broader relevance to life in general.

In the previous chapter, Steve was writing an essay about receiving a go-cart for his birthday. His essay contains a page of vivid details, but he has not yet taken the step of discovering the meaning of the piece, the "So what?" as Nancie Atwell calls it. As he was brainstorming his list of details earlier, I spotted two that could point to the importance of the go-cart in Steve's life. I mentally noted them, planning to revisit them once most of the details were in place. (Refer to the brainstorming list on page 22.) In the following conversation, I question Steve about those details.

Finding Theme

Ms. P: Okay Steve, you've got over a page of wonderful details about your go-cart, and now it's time to take it all one step further. You need a theme. Do you remember what that is?

Steve: Uh . . .

Ms. P: It's the real meaning behind the piece, the deeper issue. If you just have a bunch of details, no matter how good the details are, it will seem a bit empty without that deeper meaning.

Steve: Okay . . .

Ms. P: Do you have that excerpt from Gary Paulsen's *Woodsong* that we looked at as a class?

Steve: I think so. *(He looks through his folder and pulls it out.)*

Ms. P: Good. Look at this last paragraph again. In the story, Paulsen confronted a bear he called Scarhead in his yard. He was ready to shoot it but let the bear go. Remember?

Steve: Uh-huh.

Ms. P: Then, at the end, Paulsen says, "I hope Scarhead is still alive." See that part? Read the sentence after that out loud for me.

Steve: "For what he taught me, I hope he lives long and is very happy because I learned then—looking up at him while he made up his mind whether or not to end me—that when it is all boiled down I am nothing more and nothing less than any other animal in the woods."

Ms. P: See how he spells out a bigger meaning? It's not just a story about him confronting a bear; it's about him seeing his place in the world. Does that make sense?

We talked about this story in the mini-lesson on theme, but I often review mini-lessons during individual conferences if needed.

Steve: Yes. He thinks he's an animal too.

Ms. P: Right! That's what he learned from this experience. See? When you write, you have to give the reader some kind of life lesson—not a moral, like "You should do this" or "You should do that," but some new twist on life through your eyes. Do you get it?

Steve: Yes, but how?

Ms. P: Well, one way is to simply have a sentence like Paulsen's, that begins with a phrase like "I learned" or "I realized" *(I write these phrases in the margin of his latest draft.)* Think about how you could finish those sentences.

Steve: Okay. But I didn't learn anything.

Ms. P: Well, let's see what we've got here. Take out your list of details you did for homework. *(He brings the brainstormed list of details to the forefront. I wanted to see those details that I thought deserved further investigation.)* Let's see . . . these two details here are most interesting to me: "time capsule" and "being in my own world." *(I star them as I speak.)* Tell me what you were thinking when you wrote them.

Steve: Well, being in the cart with the bars all around feels like your own time capsule or space capsule. You're in your own space. Everything else seems like it's far away—not totally gone, but it can't touch you.

Ms. P: Interesting. And you said before it is loud, right? So I bet that makes you feel isolated, too. Like the neighbor waving—you can see him but not hear him. He doesn't completely reach you.

Steve: Yeah.

Ms. P: Do you enjoy that feeling?

Steve: Yes! I can forget about school and homework and all that stuff and just ride.

Ms. P: Okay, these ideas are very important, Steve. Write down what you just described to me, about being in your own space, apart from everyone, and feeling protected from the outside pressures in your life, like school.

Just write down what you said. Put "having my own space" and "everything seems far away." Then write down "pressures" and list the two you mentioned, homework and school.

I often find such symbolism in the students' writing. Sometimes I will point the symbols out to the student; sometimes I will just let them be and enjoy them myself. They seem mostly coincidental, but I don't think they are. The mind remembers details that are meaningful, even if the writer doesn't consciously know why.

Steve: Okay. *(He writes these phrases at the bottom of his draft.)*

Ms. P: Not now, but later, try to add to this list of pressures. Are there any others that you feel? Teachers, friends, money, anything—see if you can come up with about two more. *(I write "Others?" at the bottom of the "Pressures" list.)*

Steve: Okay.

Ms. P: Now, here's what I'm thinking: The go-cart isn't just a go-cart; it's a moment of freedom from all the pressures of your daily life. Do you agree?

In a fragile moment like this, where the student feels insecure but hasn't totally shut down, I will do this bit of handholding and dictate the exact phrases I want him to use to think about theme. Still, they are his own words, with my addition of "pressures" instead of his word "stuff."

He's looking a bit doubtful and uncomfortable, but he knows I am giving him the "answer" to theme. I purposely rephrased his ideas into more eloquent words, both as a modeling technique and as a bit of free help that he can choose to use or not.

Steve: Yes. *(As I'm speaking, I add "freedom" underneath his phrase "having my own space.")*

Ms. P: And you said your uncle gave it to you. Was it just from him?

Steve: No, he actually just brought it because my parents didn't have a hiding spot for it. It was from everyone, but mostly my parents.

Ms. P: Okay. So your parents gave you this bit of freedom to enjoy, right? Why do you think they did that?

Steve: Um . . . they want me to be happy on my birthday? I don't know.

Ms. P: Definitely, Steve! Definitely they want you to be happy. Here's what I think: You've been working hard lately, right? You've gotten your homework sheet signed every day for months, you've been doing your homework, and your grades have improved. Right?

Now he's really feeling cornered. His tone with the disclaimer "I don't know" is like a red flag. I need to encourage him and give him some options out of this, without letting up on finding a theme.

Steve: Uh, yeah.

Ms. P: I bet they feel proud of you. I bet they wanted to show you that they know you're working hard and that they're proud of you. And that you deserve a break now and then from the pressure. Don't you think?

Steve: My dad did say something like that during the cake.

Ms. P: He did? Well, you should definitely put that in the story. What did he say?

Steve: He just said, "We're proud of you."

Ms. P: That's it, Steve! That's the theme. It was there all along! Now, you just have to put it in words at the end. You can put your dad's quote in at the cake part. *(I write "Dad's quote" in the margin of the paragraph about the cake.)* But at the end, spell it out for us.

Steve: How?

Ms. P: Well, right here, after you use the time capsule simile, start a paragraph explaining more about how the go-cart made you feel. Then explain the pressures. Then start a few sentences with "I learned" or one of those phrases.

> *Steve's dad may have said more, but I won't press Steve on it. I'll see what turns up in the story.*

> *Again, I purposely say "after you use the time capsule simile" instead of "after you talk about the time capsule" or "after the time capsule part." I write "1" over the notes about having his own space, "2" next to the "Pressures" list, and "3" next to the theme starter phrases I jotted earlier on his draft.*

He added a paragraph before his final paragraph. It read:

> *Riding the go-cart made me feel free, like I had my own space. Everything felt far away, like school, homework, money worries, and my sister. I realized my parents knew how hard I was working at school and were proud of me.*

It wasn't much more than we had discussed, but it was enough. Many students do not need as much direction as Steve did; they will run with the idea of theme once they see a few examples and understand its purpose. Even for Steve, writing with thematic intention will be much easier in future papers. The key is consistency. I grade students on theme in every paper, even though it will take a different form depending on the genre. This way, students develop the habit of always looking for a deeper layer in their essays.

AUTOBIOGRAPHY

Developing Theme

My next conversation is with Lauren. There is a hint of a theme in her first draft, but it needs to be identified and fleshed out. The paper first looks like this:

> *My dad had decided to take my brother and I on a canoe ride to see the fireworks. We had to park the car in front of someone else's house, and ask their permission to go into the water from their backyard. They said yes, but were reluctant to let us do so, since it was almost dark. My dad and brother had to carry the canoe, so all I had to do was hold the flashlight on their path. I was glad about that because I wouldn't want to be carrying a canoe in the dark. We had to step over a wire to get into the water, and then step onto a small rickety bridge, which was only big enough to hold one person at a time. Then, we started to paddle out into the middle of the lake. Actually, I didn't have to paddle the canoe, so I just stared up at the night sky, waiting for the fireworks to begin.*

I didn't feel like saying anything because I had argued with my dad earlier that day about going out with my friends. My dad reassured my brother and I that this was a good view, but we were skeptic. All of a sudden, we heard cheering from the shores, where families were having parties. The fireworks had started, and my dad had been right. We had the best view in the town. Everywhere you looked in the sky, there were fireworks of all shapes and sizes. There were sparkles, shimmers, explosions, squiggly lines and even smiley faces. We saw every firework twice—once in the sky and once in the water.

On the shores all around us, people were setting off their own firecrackers, competing to see who had the most, and whose "show" was better. They were extremely loud and very brightly colored. The crackling of the firecrackers and beauty of the fireworks was stunning. The experience I had was wonderful. As the finale came to an end, I leaned over toward my dad and said, "Thanks."

I know Lauren had already brainstormed some details before writing the piece. I could push her for more, but I was more interested in the fact that she had argued with her father earlier that day about going out with friends that night.

Ms. P: Lauren, you have some nice details here, like how you held the flashlight in the path, and how you stepped over a wire and crossed a rickety bridge. *(I star them.)* Also, you have a good bit of onomatopoeia with the word "crackling." *(Star.)* I really feel like I can imagine those moments, like I'm there. *(Praise.)*

Lauren: Thanks.

Ms. P: Tell me more about the argument earlier that day. You had wanted to do something else that night?

Lauren: Yes. I wanted to go out with Amy and Kristen to watch fireworks, but my dad insisted that my brother and me go with him.

Ms. P: What was the argument like?

Lauren: I don't know, just a regular argument.

> *I can tell she thinks this is irrelevant, but she is willing to go along with it.*

Ms. P: What's that like? Did it get loud? Did you say anything you regretted?

Lauren: Well, yeah, I was yelling and said some stuff. But I gave in.

Ms. P: Yes, yes—I'm not saying you're at fault in any way, Lauren. All kids fight with their parents. What I'm thinking is this: There might be more to this story than you're letting on. So far, you have some nice description about the canoe and the fireworks. Then at the end you thank your dad. But that's it. A description of fireworks is nice, but for an essay you want to dig a bit deeper. Let's look around for a theme. Were you angry at your dad after the argument?

Lauren: For a while I was.

Ms. P: In the boat, were you? It seems like you were because—here—you "didn't want to say anything."

Lauren: Yes, but I forgot all about it when the fireworks started.

Ms. P: Right. To me, this story seems to be about the fireworks, yes, but also about forgiving your dad for not letting you do what you wanted to do. Don't you think?

Lauren: I don't know, maybe.

Ms. P: Let's just imagine that part of this story is about forgetting about that fight. It would make the essay stronger and take it to the next level. It's not unusual or strange or anything: An adolescent argues with her dad, gives in, and then lets it go. It's actually a sign of maturity. And you say yourself in the piece that the fireworks were amazing and he was right about watching them from the lake, right?

Lauren: Yeah. Watching them from the canoe was great.

Ms. P: Okay, so try this: In the middle here, where you mention the argument, make it into its own paragraph instead. Describe what happened, what was said, and how you felt. Then, just imagine in your mind that out on the lake with your dad you let go of any negative feelings. How would that feel? What would you do? Also, I want you to just imagine floating in the canoe, and write down any details about those moments: sights, sounds, smells, physical feelings, the lights—right before the fireworks.

> *I'm pushing her, but trying to pull back by saying, "Let's imagine." It lets her off the hook, for now, of owning up to her feelings. We're "imagining" forgiveness, as if we were building a piece of fiction.*

> *Students are often reluctant to go beyond simple description. If she hadn't mentioned the fight, I would have still steered her in the direction of her father, suggesting that she look more deeply into how she feels about him. Maybe while sitting in the canoe, she realizes how much she appreciates him and that she sometimes takes him for granted. Maybe she is grateful that he has different ideas than everyone else and isn't afraid to make the effort to implement them. I don't want her to lie or exaggerate; I want her to look more closely at what's already there. I refrain from saying that water can be a symbol for cleansing and renewal, or that the journey to the water carrying the burden of the canoe on their shoulders is also potentially symbolic; perhaps when the piece is finished I will tell her how intuitive her writing is, but for now, I don't want to confuse or intimidate her.*

Lauren: Okay.

Ms. P: This will also help get you beyond one page. Think you can try it?

Lauren: Yes. Okay.

> *My final argument for writing a theme: It will bring the paper to the required length. Most students, even if they think adding a theme is unnecessary, will try anything to get to a page since that directly contributes to their overall grade on the piece. I finish this conference with a question so that she realizes that ultimately the piece depends on her memory, her feelings, and her willingness to write, that she is in control.*

> *I jot down notes in the margins: "Paragraph for argument," "Forgiving Dad—feelings? Actions?" At the top of the page I write, "Canoe: sights, light, sounds, smells, touch." I don't want to overload her, but sometimes, having an "easy" task like remembering some details can ease the discomfort of trying to find a theme; the mind has something tangible to work on while the theme ripens.*

When I check on her again, I see a paragraph about her dad right after the first paragraph. It reads:

> *I wasn't in a great mood. I didn't feel like saying anything because I had argued with my dad earlier that day about going out with my friends. I had wanted to go watch the fireworks with Kristen and Amy, but my dad insisted that my brother and me go with him. I didn't like how it is always his way or the high way. As I stared at the water, I could see small bugs darting to and fro across the surface. There was a cool breeze blowing, but I didn't feel cold. We drifted for a while silently, hearing the sounds of voices from parties along the shores.*

Ms. P: Great job, Lauren! Your additions are excellent.

Lauren: Thanks.

Ms. P: Now, let's look at the theme. You really nailed it right here: "I don't like how it is always his way or the high way." "Highway" should be one word. *(I connect the word on her paper with a curved underline.)* But I don't want you to use it anyway. It's a cliché. We say it all the time. Do you know what I mean by that? It's like saying, "It's raining cats and dogs." Everyone always says it. Your job as a writer is to say it a different way, the exact way for you. In your own words.

Lauren: Okay.

Ms. P: But the idea of it is perfect. Don't change that. Just reword it. *(I underline the sentence and write "reword" in the margin.)* Then I want you to add just one more sentence which will help take the theme one small step further. *(I'm trying to minimize the task a bit so she's not discouraged or intimidated.)* This part right here—"my dad had been right"—is very important, because I think it has a double meaning. He was right about the spot being the best spot, but he was also right about it being more important that you were all together that night, because he had this great surprise planned. Do you agree?

> Students are often pleasantly surprised to find out they wrote something that can have two meanings, so I point out these instances to them whenever I can.

Lauren: Yes—I didn't even mean that to have a double meaning.

Ms. P: That's alright. Sometimes our minds are smarter than we are. It happens to writers all the time.

Lauren: Really? It seems like it doesn't count if I didn't do it on purpose.

Ms. P: Everything counts. Even if you didn't originally intend to do it, you still wrote it; they're your words. Your choice now is to ignore it or run with it. In order to own it and be in control of the whole piece, you have to think it through.

Lauren: Okay, but how?

Ms. P: Add a sentence to the end of this paragraph. *(I put an asterisk in the spot.)* Spell out what you were thinking. Start with "I realized" or "I knew then" or "I learned." Finish that thought. What did you realize about your dad at that moment? What did you feel? Tell it exactly. You can write more than one sentence if you want. That part will be the heart of the essay.

> I make those questions rhetorical ones; I rarely ask them in a way that expects the student to vocalize an answer on the spot. Adolescents would hate that, I think. Instead, I write the starter phrases in the margin near the asterisk and let her mull them over. I'm careful to resist writing the sentence for her.

Lauren: Okay.

When I check back, she has printed a draft with all the changes implemented so far:

My dad had decided to take my brother and I on a canoe ride to see the fireworks. We had to park the car in front of someone else's house, and ask their permission to go into the water from their backyard. They said yes, but were reluctant to let us do so, since it was almost dark. My dad and brother had to carry the canoe, so all I had to do was hold the flashlight on their path. I was glad about that because I wouldn't want to be carrying a canoe in the dark. We had to step over a wire to get into the water, and then step onto a small rickety bridge, which was only big enough to hold one person at a time. Then, we started to paddle out into the middle of the lake. Actually, I didn't have to paddle the canoe, so I just stared up at the night sky, waiting for the fireworks to begin.

I wasn't in a great mood. I didn't feel like saying anything because I had argued with my dad earlier about going out that day with my friends. I had wanted to go watch the fireworks with Kristen and Amy, but my dad insisted that my brother and me go with him. I didn't like how he treats me like I'm still a child like my brother. As I stared at the water, I could see small bugs darting to and fro across the surface. There was a cool breeze blowing, but I didn't feel cold. We drifted for a while silently, hearing the sounds of voices from parties along the shores.

My dad reassured my brother and I that this was a good view, but we were skeptical. All of a sudden, we heard cheering from the shores, where families were having parties. The fireworks had started, and my dad had been right. We had the best view in the town. Everywhere you looked in the sky, there were fireworks of all shapes and sizes. There were sparkles, shimmers, explosions, squiggly lines and even smiley faces. We saw every firework twice—once in the sky and once in the water. I realized then that my dad had planned this nice surprise for me and my brother, and he just wanted to share it with us.

On the shores all around us, people were setting off their own firecrackers, competing to see who had the most, and whose "show" was better. They were extremely loud and very brightly colored. The crackling of the firecrackers and beauty of the fireworks was stunning. The experience I had was wonderful. As the finale came to an end, I leaned over toward my dad and saw the lights flashing on his face. I even saw tiny fireworks reflected in his eyes. He looked at me, smiling, and I said, "Thanks."

Ms. P: Excellent! This is it exactly, Lauren. Now the whole essay has depth and meaning. I see that you also added a wonderful detail at the end: the fireworks flashing on your dad's face. That is really just a stroke of genius! Great work.

Lauren: Thanks. As I was reading it, I remembered that and put it in.

Ms. P: Well, it's perfect. Nice work.

The last major step I will conference with Lauren about is the introduction. For that, she will be able to use what she already has, with a bit of rearranging. I always like to have the theme of the piece done first so the student knows the essay's destination.

CHARACTER SKETCH

Weaving In Theme

A character sketch is a rudimentary but effective exercise that helps students learn to write with the intention of theme. After a thorough prewrite, students write rich, vivid descriptions of people in their lives. I then ask them to end the piece with some thoughts about why the person is important to them, what they have learned from the person, or how they have changed because of that person. I have found that for some reason, students are not afraid to write freely about their chosen subject; to admit that one's parent, sibling, or best friend has affected one's life is not risky or even difficult. Students are often relieved that they can tackle such a nebulous concept as theme with so straightforward a technique. A setting sketch can also serve as an effective way to practice thematic development.

Below is one student's character sketch about his older brother. He already has an interesting idea for an introduction (the guidelines for the assignment suggested using a scene to frame the entire piece and act as a scaffold for the details), but he wasn't quite sure how to word the theme and where to weave it in.

As I walked into the laundry room looking for my soccer uniform for a game that I had later that day, I noticed the scent of fabric softener and the sound of the dryer shaking. My brother was sitting on the washing machine reading a Sports Illustrated magazine. He told me that his clothes were almost finished as I walked by him. My brother, Chris, is a tall, muscular 17 year old with dark skin and dark hair. Chris is fun to be around because he makes everyone laugh. Chris is a normal high school student. He plays football, gets average grades, has a lot of friends, and spikes his hair every day.

While I sat on the ground rummaging through tons of Chris's clothes, I looked up at him and thought about how weird it was for him to do his own laundry. And because he has so many clothes, he is always in the laundry room; it's like his second bedroom. He usually likes to wear jeans and T-shirts layered on top of each other. Sometimes he wears two short sleeve shirts, or a short sleeve over a long sleeve. It adds up to a lot of shirts and jeans.

Chris is a big fan of rap music and sometimes tries to make up his own rhymes but they never come out too well. He also has a strange laugh that gets annoying (it sounds like a pig), but I have gotten used to it and just ignore it.

When I finally find my jersey, I tell him that I have found it. The only word that he says is "Bueno." Bueno is Spanish for good and it's been a word that he's said for a couple months now. I rolled my eyes at him and he smiled his large smile and went back to reading.

Ms. P: John, this is wonderful—you have so many interesting details about Chris: the spiked hair, the clothes, the rapping, the "bueno." And the scene that you chose seems very natural.

John: He's really always there.

Ms. P: I can tell! How's the theme coming?

John: Well, I understand the questions about why the person is important, but I don't know where to put it.

Ms. P: Let's see—you're in the laundry room, you find your jersey at the end—why not put it at the end there? In a piece of memoir like this character sketch, usually the theme is going to be expressed as a thought in your head. So you can think it whenever you want. You could think it when you are rummaging through the laundry, but you're already thinking something else at that point. I would say, go for the ending.

John: So . . . I just put, "I think about how my brother has helped me," or something like that?

Ms. P: Something like that. You can try to weave it into the scene: You found your jersey, and you will probably be walking out of the room. So you could have him say one more thing and that makes you think it, or you could just look at him and think it, or you could just walk out and think it. It doesn't have to be much—just tie it to the scene in some small way so that it doesn't feel like a patch you just stuck on the piece.

John: Okay. I'll try it.

When I next read John's paper, I see that he added the following sentences to the last paragraph:

> *When I finally find my jersey, I tell him that I have found it. The only word that he says is "Bueno." Bueno is Spanish for good and it's been a word that he's said for a couple months now. I rolled my eyes at him and he smiled his large smile and went back to reading. On my way out of the laundry room I look back at my brother and think about all he has taught and shown me over the years. And I never forget how he protects me when I am in trouble. He is always watching over me and I respect him for that.*

As always, I am trying to communicate that writing is a made thing, an art, an artifice, and the writer makes choices according to what's best for the piece. In the assignment guidelines for the character sketch, I instructed the students to choose a scene that happened, or could have happened. Or maybe it's a scene that often happens, and the writer has to create one instance from a multitude of occurrences. And the theme need not be something that the student actually thought at a particular moment; it can be some broader truth that he inserts into this particular moment.

Ms. P: John, this is excellent. I love how you're walking out and look back at him. It's a very natural part of the piece. Well done.

John: Thanks. You said to make it seem natural.

Ms. P: And you did it on the first try, John. Really great. Now, there's one major thing you have to fix with the grammar—it's major but it's easy to fix. Then you can hand it in.

John: Okay. What is it?

Ms. P: Well, look at your first sentence. What's the verb?

John: Um . . . "walked"?

Ms. P: That's one of them, yes. *(I circle it.)* Let's put this whole clause aside though for a second. *(I put parentheses around the entire first dependent clause.)* Okay, start from here. What's the main verb of the sentence?

John: "Noticed."

Ms. P: Right. Look at these two verbs. What tense are they in?

John: The . . . uh . . . past.

Ms. P: Right. Now, look at the first sentence in your last paragraph. Where's the verb?

John: "Find?"

That's twice now that he picked the verb in the dependent clause instead of the main verb in the sentence. I decide to deviate from my original grammar lesson on tense to show him the difference between independent and dependent clauses.

Ms. P: Well, it's the same situation here as the first sentence—you have a dependent clause and an independent clause. It's what I call a two-part sentence. The first part can't be alone, but the second part can if it wanted to. *(I draw a line after "jersey.")* See? The first part is "When I finally find my jersey" and the second is "I tell him that I have found it." The first can't be alone. Imagine if I just went up to you and said, "When I finally find my jersey." *(As I say this, my facial expression is one of exaggerated anticipation. Then I pause.)*

John: Yeah?

Ms. P: Right. You're waiting for the rest of the thought. That's why it can't be alone. But the other half can—it's a complete thought. Get it?

John: Yes.

Ms. P: You usually need a special word in a two-part sentence for the dependent half. See the poster about it above Jamie's head? What are some of the two-part words?

I often direct students to refer to various posters around the room. One has a long list of words that could potentially appear in a two-part sentence.

John: "When," "while," "as," "although," "because"—

Ms. P: Right. And look at your first sentence. What word do you use to introduce your dependent clause?

John: Um . . . "As."

Ms. P: Right. Now, the reason I'm telling you all this is not because you made a mistake with dependent clauses; actually you're quite good with them—I see you used one to start your third paragraph as well. You could throw a comma in the middle of the sentence if you wanted, especially if it's a long sentence—but grammatically they're correct.

John: Okay.

Ms. P: But if I ask you what the verb of the sentence is, you have to find the verb in the *independent* clause, or *main* clause, as we call it. Just now when I twice asked you for the verbs in those sentences, you just said the first verb you found, when what you should be looking for is the main verb of the whole sentence.

I wouldn't do this grammar lesson within a grammar lesson with all students, as it could be confusing. John, however, can handle it, and since he made the same mistake in verb identification twice, I thought it best to detour from my original purpose for a minute, especially since his essay lent itself to several examples.

John: Okay.

Ms. P: Alright, so let me ask you again about this sentence beginning your last paragraph: What's the verb? Look at the *main* clause, the *independent* clause.

John: Um . . . "tell"?

Ms. P: Excellent. Now, what tense is "tell"?

John: Uh . . .

Ms. P: Today I tell, yesterday I told, tomorrow I will tell—

John: Oh! Present.

Ms. P: Do you see where I'm headed with this?

John: Um . . .

Ms. P: Look at your first verb, "noticed," and this verb, "tell." What's the difference?

I am drawing it out, but I want him to find it himself. Hopefully, investing the time now will save me time later because he will check his verbs himself; even if he doesn't, I can just write "verb tense" in the margin and he'll know what to do.

John: Oh! I switched from past to present.

Ms. P: Right. It's extremely common to do that; everyone does it at one point or another, even adult writers who have been writing for some time. Now, let me show you how it happened. See this third paragraph, where you talk about characteristics about Chris that are always true, like how he likes rap and has a strange laugh?

John: Yes. Those are in the present.

Ms. P: Right, and they should be, because you're describing things that are true long-term— he still likes rap, right? And he still has a strange laugh, even now, right?

John: Definitely.

Ms. P: So those should be in the present, because they're always true. But the scene— the laundry room action—should be in the past. So, do you see what you did? You switched to the present for the always-true statements, and then you never switched back to the past when you came back to the laundry room in the last paragraph. Very easy mistake to do, but you have to be on the lookout for it.

John: Oh, right, okay.

Ms. P: So we're really only talking about a couple verbs here, because even in the last paragraph, you have statements that are always true, so they should be in the present. Pick out only the "laundry room" verbs, circle them, and put them in the past. Do you understand?

John: Yes, yes. I can do that.

Ms. P: Good. Then print a fresh copy and hand it in. For the next few assignments, I want you to include "verb tense" on your E/R Check Sheets.

John: Okay.

Ms. P: Great job on this one, John. You should show your brother when you're done.

John: Thanks—maybe I'll show him.

For each assignment, the students must complete an Editing/Revising Check Sheet as a final step before submitting the piece for grading. The Editing/Revising Check Sheets change each quarter, but they always have a space for the individual student to add his particular problem area to check. Sample Editing/Revising Check Sheets are included in Teaching Students to Write Effective Essays.

When I grade the paper, I'll see if John was able to tease out the "laundry room" verbs in that last paragraph, and if he realized the word *now* would have to be changed as well. At any rate, he put so much work into the content that it seemed like a short lesson in verbs and clauses would stick. In future assignments with John, I will try to reinforce what we discussed and purposely use the terms *dependent clause* and *independent clause*.

Finally, when grading John's paper, I will circle the three phrases "Chris is" in his first paragraph and write "Change 2" in the margin; when he sees it, John will remember our class rule about not starting more than one sentence in a paragraph the same way. Since I think he can figure that out himself, I didn't mention it during our conferences for the sake of time.

Finding Theme in an Expository Essay

Here is one short conversation I had with a student working on a How-To essay about making a layup. This type of essay is more explanatory and directed than a memoir; however, it still needs a reason for the reader to read it.

Melani had all the steps for executing a successful layup already mapped and written in paragraphs, with appropriate transition words throughout. When I reached her desk, she was puzzling over the theme.

Melani: Isn't a theme about things like "surviving" and "don't cheat" and stuff like that?

Ms. P: Well, in stories—fiction and memoir—it can be, but other kinds of essays can have themes too.

Melani: How? It's not a story. It's just instructions on how to do something.

Ms. P: They are just instructions if you leave them the way they are. But you can give the whole essay another dimension by explaining why it is important. It's not just about doing a layup; it's about you living your life. Doing a layup is part of your life—don't you agree?

Melani: Definitely. I wouldn't be on the team without it.

Ms. P: That's it exactly, Melani. So this essay is not just about lifting your left knee when you are shooting from the left; it's about your learning something about yourself, and about life. Your job as a writer is to explain what that is.

Melani: Okay, but how?

Ms. P: Ask yourself these questions: What did I learn about myself in this process? How has this changed my life? How have I grown as a person? What did I learn about life in general? *(Even though these questions were listed on the assignment sheet, I jot down key phrases from each on her paper.)* Think you can do that?

Melani: Yes.

Ms. P: Take your time; mull it over for a bit. If you get stuck, raise your hand, but otherwise, you can just use the theme as your conclusion.

> An instruction manual does not need a theme, but an essay does.

> *This strategy is a first step in trying to get the student to link the topic to a larger perspective. It can be used with any type of essay. With memoir it is obvious; however, with, say, a persuasive essay, I would ask, "Feeling strongly about lowering the working age is a part of your life right now, don't you think?" If the student can see the impact of the topic on his life, then he can start to verbalize its importance; if expressed effectively, it becomes important to the reader as well.*

Melani worked on the essay for another class or two, finishing the theme and working on other aspects of the paper. I included her complete essay in *Teaching Students to Write Effective Essays;* the last two paragraphs of the essay appear below.

Learning this has helped me more than I expected. First, when I couldn't do a layup, I never scored any points, or even helped my team out that much. Then, my dad taught me how to do it, and it was so easy that I started teaching other girls that didn't know how. I was so proud of myself for working at it, and getting it down pat. This made me grow as a basketball player, and be stronger. I don't mean physically stronger.

I could associate with my teammates when I never could do that before. Now we talk all the time, and I am very outgoing, and willing to help people with skills, or just even introduce myself to a new kid. Once I got through a game with about 16 points just from layups. I have grown to be a better basketball player, and I have much more confidence too.

Melani took the essay to a deeper level by making it about confidence, generosity of self, and even (unbeknownst to her, perhaps) her relationship with her dad. These are ideas that, besides being meaningful and interesting, most readers can relate to. They make her essay more than merely a list of steps or a sports story.

All topics can be transformed in this way. I have even seen students deepen that most elementary of subjects, making a peanut butter sandwich (a topic I try to discourage by eighth grade), into an essay about responsibility, growing up, or connecting with a loved one who taught the age-old skill. At the same time, if students feel silly about making such a "big deal" about a certain topic, perhaps they haven't chosen a topic in which they have enough emotional investment. Writing with thematic intention often pushes students to select subjects that lend themselves to deeper thought and personal meaningfulness.

CHAPTER 6

Jumbled Ideas: Instilling Organization

Like many other complications that crop up in the writing of a piece, disorganization can be substantially reduced with thoughtful prewriting and planning. Prewriting, of course, can take many forms, but all prewriting should incorporate a second step in which those early ideas are organized. For example, a lengthy brainstorming list should be weeded and grouped; a freewrite should be cracked open and the main ideas extracted and ordered. I've always felt that one pitfall of webbing is that the web can often appear organized when it is not; a second, rearranged web would better serve the student. Whatever the technique, the more thought the student puts in during the prewriting stage, the clearer the drafts will be. For this reason, I spend several mini-lessons explaining ways to organize a prewrite, and I make "Grouping" part of the final grade in the "Prewriting" category of the rubric.

Having said that, I should add that I have only one set rule for how essays should be organized: they should be logical and purposefully done. Certain essays lend themselves to certain structures, and I present those structures in each essay's mini-lessons, but I do not reject alternative structures if they make sense and are purposefully employed by the writer. Few middle school students will intentionally experiment with structure, since often they are writing in the genres for the first time and they feel most comfortable following instructions precisely. This is fine with me; I've always believed that one should be familiar with the traditional forms before attempting to deviate from them. However, with each assignment, after I explain an "easy" organizational method to my students, I always add that they, as writers, can try something different if they choose. This communicates to them that form is malleable and that the writer controls it. Sometimes, as with a compare-and-contrast essay, I offer two organizational structures and tell the students to choose the one that best suits their style and content. With all prewrites, I instruct students to group their thoughts and order them "in a way that seems best to you." They know that they must present their ideas logically, but they can determine for themselves the most effective arrangement.

> Whatever the scheme, an essay's organization should be (1) logical and (2) purposefully done.

I often suggest more sophisticated structures during individual conferences when I think both the essay and the writer can handle it. For example, I will sometimes help a student use a flashback in order to create a compelling introduction for an autobiographical piece.

Major Cutting and Rearranging of Ideas

A significant cause of poor organization is overgeneralizing and the repetition of those generalizations. In the following example, Mark does just that in his personal essay, an assignment meant to be a somewhat philosophical reflection on a topic. He has some general ideas about his subject, paintball, but not enough specific detail to anchor the structure as a whole, so the piece jumps from one idea to another.

On Paintball

Paintball is an extreme sport in which a player shoots a capsule full of paint through a gun at an opponent. Of the many extreme sports of today paintball is the most exciting. There are many important and certain educational aspects of the sport. There are also many fun aspects of the sport too. Its a sport that teaches courage, bravery and strategy. It may be one of the most educational sports.

It is one of my favorite pastimes and the favorite pastime of many other people I know. It's fun because its like when you were a little kid and played with toy guns but this brings it up a level. It lets the child inside you come out at more of a professional level. Its easy to learn and can be played almost anywhere. You have to strategize and make a plan. It's also a sport that teaches teamwork. I know this for a fact because I was out paintballing with my friend and we had to work together to advance. I would cover him as he moved up to the next bunker and then he would cover me. Without working in a team you would never accomplish your goal.

It is a sport that is very easy to get into. You can play it just about anywhere with a bunch of space. It is always very exciting. There are also many specialized areas to play paintball. No matter where you go though paintball is always fun. Beginners can have a great time too. They just stay on the rec. ball side of things. I went paintballing with my dad and he had no idea what he was doing but he caught on quick and had an unbelievable time.

There are two levels to the sport of paintball, recreational and tournament. Both levels have their ups and downs. Rec. ball is fun and challenging. But you usually have a lot of "newbies" playing. Tournament ball is played on small fields with high speed guns. Most of the players that play here are on a very advanced level. On the up side there are sometimes a few prizes.

No matter what level you play at or where you play paintball is fun. It requires some skill and is very demanding but "he that can't endure the bad will not live to see the good." (Anonymous)

This is one of those papers that makes me sigh over the amount of work needed. I don't usually get discouraged, but I do feel overwhelmed sometimes. The editor in me wants to change almost everything about this paper: the use of the second person, the repetition, the lack of detail, the language, the lack of sentence variation, the introduction, and the conclusion. First, Mark must weed out the repetition, see what actual ideas are left, arrange them purposefully and strategically, and fill in more details.

Ms. P: Mark, you clearly know a lot about your subject—good choice of topic. You obviously feel passionate about paintball!

Mark: I do—it's awesome. I play almost every weekend.

Ms. P: How long have you been playing?

Mark: Um . . . maybe a couple years now.

Ms. P: Wow—do you ever play in those tournaments you mentioned?

Mark: Sometimes. They're really high-level and mostly older kids dominate them. But I did win a prize once.

Ms. P: Really? That's impressive!

Mark: It was just a small gift certificate to a local sports store, but it was fun to get.

Ms. P: I'm sure it was. How often are there tournaments?

Mark: Around here, maybe one every other month. They're small. But if you're willing to travel, you could go to more.

Ms. P: How interesting! I never knew it was so popular. I thought it was just a recreational game people did occasionally. I had no idea it is an actual sport.

Mark: Oh yeah, people are really serious about it. And there's all kinds of equipment—it can get pretty expensive.

Ms. P: Well, it's clear that you have a lot of experience. Let's look at what you have so far in the paper. You have the makings here for a powerful essay if you can move some parts around a bit and add more details.

> *I invest some time in the conversation about paintball not only out of genuine interest, but also to show Mark that I care about what's important to him, and that he is the expert here. I want him to be motivated for the work that lies ahead, the amount of which I deliberately downplayed.*

Mark: Okay.

Ms. P: Let's look at your groups. Did you do any groups or an outline or web or something?

Mark: Right here. *(As I suspected, it was done quickly and generally.)*

Paintball

feelings—fun!

skills—teamwork, courage, strategy

places—anywhere, special areas

levels—rec, tournament

quote—??

Ms. P: Okay, so you have some general ideas. What's missing right from the start, Mark, are the details—the sights, the sounds, the smells, the feeling of a paintball smacking your back. *(He smiles.)* Right! See what I'm saying? As the reader, I want to know those details. I want to feel like I'm there. Now, look what happens when you don't use details. You start to repeat the same general terms over and over. Look at your first paragraph. Can you figure out what idea gets repeated there?

Mark: Um . . . *(He reads.)* Oh! It's educational?

Ms. P: Right. You repeat "educational," but in the paper you never explain how paintball actually *is* educational. Now, go through your paper, and circle all the times you use the word "fun."

Mark: Okay. *(I wait.)* Um . . . one, two, three, four. Four.

Ms. P: Right. Four times is a lot for a word like "fun" in a one-page paper. It's not specific. You know what I think of when I think of fun? Going to a poetry reading. Is paintball like that?

Mark: Uh . . . no?

Ms. P: I didn't think so. You need to find words that capture the exact feeling. Or better yet, describe it so well that I feel like I'm there and I can feel the feeling myself. Let's start with that. I'm going to make some categories here. *(I list the senses on his outline sheet.)* I want you to close your eyes and imagine you're paintballing. Then, for each category, I want you to write at least two or three details. Then I'll check back. Okay?

Mark: Mmm hmm. *(His eyes are already closed.)*

When I return, I find that Mark has in fact come up with a number of engaging sensory details about playing paintball. With this list, his original draft, and his original outline on his desk, we continue our conversation.

sights—trees, trails, clothes splattered like a painting by that famous guy

sounds—whiz of paintballs, pop of guns, feet running

smells—trees, outdoors, paint?

touch—sting of paint capsule as it hits, branches scratching

taste—sweat

Ms. P: Excellent work, Mark. I especially like the onomatopoeia in words like "whiz," and "pop"— the sound is the word. Do you see how these details are so much more interesting for the reader than simply saying "fun" four times?

Mark: Yes.

Ms. P: Okay, let's look at your original outline. *(He brings it to the forefront.)* You have many of these ideas from the outline in your draft, but they're a bit mixed together and general. In the outline, instead of "fun," let's make that a paragraph about the details of the experience.

Mark: Okay.

Ms. P: So cross out "feelings—fun!" and write "experience." *(He does.)* Good. Let's look at the rest of them. Do you still want to keep all of these? Are there any you might not need?

Mark: Well, I put a quote at the end since it was part of the assignment grade, but I don't know if it fits.

Ms. P: Yes, I was thinking that same thing. You have good instincts. *(Genuine praise!)* Let's put the quote on hold until we get the other paragraphs shaped up. Instead, for that last paragraph, you might want to try a theme. Do you have a theme already, do you think? An answer for the reader's question of "Why should I care?"

Mark: Well . . . they should care because it's fun?

Ms. P: Well, yes, the details you came up with will definitely make the reader interested. But is there some other reason, something about paintball that makes it important in life?

Mark: Maybe . . . that it requires teamwork . . . and courage?

Ms. P: Yes! See? You had the theme in your original outline, but it didn't get very far in your paper. Save that idea for your conclusion—write "conclusion" next to it in the outline. *(He does.)* Good. Now, what do you think about the rest of the outline? Should any of these be combined or cut?

Mark: Well, there's only two left and I don't want to cut them. I guess I should put them in one paragraph?

Ms. P: I think so. That way you could have a paragraph about the technical aspects of the sport. *(He draws a bracket at the side of the terms and writes "combine" beside it.)* Good. Now, what order should everything go in?

Mark: Well, the details first, then the technical stuff, then the conclusion. *(He numbers them in his outline.)*

Ms. P: Excellent. Let me suggest one more idea: save some of your exciting details for the introduction. Check your notebook for introduction techniques that use details. Remember? *(I often refer students to notes taken during mini-lessons.)*

Mark: Oh, yeah, like "Imagine a paintball hitting you"?

Ms. P: Yes, something like that. You decide. *(I write "See notebook for introduction" on the outline.)* Now since you're going to be rewriting much of this, I want you to open a new document and start on a clean page. Don't try to revise your old draft—you might get stuck in it.

Mark: You mean I can't use anything I wrote before?

Ms. P: No—you can save anything you think is worth it. Here's what I want you to do: get scissors and cut out anything interesting from your old draft. Do it in one- or two-sentence chunks—don't cut a whole paragraph since every paragraph has something flat in it, like the word "fun" or something like that. Avoid any sentences with "fun" or "exciting" in them. Just cut out the really interesting parts. Then take your cutouts and put them in piles so they follow the new outline. Then toss the rest.

Mark: Okay.

Ms. P: Let me know when you've done that and I'll check in.

Manually separating the wheat from the chaff will give Mark a visual representation of how much fluff and repetition he had in his first draft. At the same time, it will preserve the ideas that are worth developing. In addition, being able to physically manipulate ideas will greatly help Mark organize them. If he were to try to open his first draft on the computer and work from that, I don't think he would be able to sort it all out as quickly or easily.

The scissors technique is also helpful with research papers and other longer papers that need to be rearranged. In these cases, even if the student does not need to delete much, it is easier to reorder longer paragraphs that span from one page to another by physically maneuvering them on a desk or floor before doing so on a computer.

After a student separates the usable ideas into piles, he can paper clip and label the piles with sticky notes to keep them in order, or put them in envelopes and label the envelopes. Or he could tape the ideas in order on clean paper. In Mark's case, since he hopefully won't have many pieces of paper (due to the amount of repetition and generalization), I'll have him use paper clips. When I return to his desk, I see the following sections removed and grouped:

EXPERIENCES/DETAILS

- Paintball is an extreme sport in which a player shoots a capsule full of paint through a gun at an opponent.
- When you were a little kid and played with toy guns but this brings it up a level. It lets the child inside you come out at more of a professional level.

TECHNICAL STUFF

- There are also many specialized areas to play paintball.
- There are two levels to the sport of paintball, recreational and tournament.
- Rec. ball is ~~fun~~ and challenging. But you usually have a lot of "newbies" playing. Tournament ball is played on small fields with high speed guns. Most of the players that play here are on a very advanced level. On the up side there are sometimes a few prizes.
- Its easy to learn and can be played almost anywhere.

CONCLUSION / THEME

- It's also a sport that teaches teamwork. I know this for a fact because I was out paintballing with my friend and we had to work together to advance. I would cover him as he moved up to the next bunker and then he would cover me. Without working in a team you would never accomplish your goal.
- Its a sport that teaches courage, bravery and strategy. It may be one of the most educational sports.

Ms. P: Excellent work, Mark. Was it difficult deciding what to keep?

Mark: No, but I wanted to keep that one sentence with "fun" in it because I needed the rest of it.

Ms. P: That's fine, Mark. You can always use your own judgment. The next step is to write up a new draft. Don't feel like you have to use these ideas word for word; you can reword and reshape them however you think sounds best. You can cut more out of them or add to them. Actually, you should probably plan on adding more details and examples wherever you can. For example, look at this idea about winning prizes—can you name a prize or two? That would be interesting for the reader.

Mark: Okay, sure. Can I write the introduction first or should I wait till the end?

Ms. P: At this point, you could certainly write the intro first since you know what you're doing.

Mark: Good, 'cause I have a great idea for it—I'm going to make it like a nature walk and then surprise you by getting hit with something, but you won't know it's a paintball till the end of the paragraph.

Ms. P: Sounds gripping, Mark. Can't wait to read it!

Nothing makes me happier in class than to see a student excited by one of his own ideas for a piece of writing. After he writes the new draft, I'll help him with sentence variation, if needed. I'm hoping that all the new details will naturally create some sentence variety. Also, I will review the difference between "it's" and "its" with Mark in a later conference.

PERSUASIVE ESSAY

Minor Trimming and Moving of Ideas

While most papers don't need as drastic an overhaul as Mark's, many of the organizational problems that crop up can be traced to the repetition of ideas where they don't belong. When we write, one thought leads to another, and even the most organized prewrites can get jumbled. In constructing the first draft of the following persuasive essay, Rob's distinct ideas became intertwined. He also has a rudimentary introduction and conclusion. Although they both need polishing, and the language in general needs strengthening, it's the organization that attracts my attention at this point.

Young or Old?

I know there is an age to begin driving but should there be an age to end it? At a younger age like 17 eyesight is keen. Your body doesn't have a problem moving the car out of the way fast enough. Teenagers also drive at a steady pace. They just took and passed their driving test so they are aware of the rules required for driving. Older people on the other hand aren't as up-to-date.

As we get older our bodies change again. Our eye sight goes and our reflexes get slower. Driving uses both those skills. Bad eye sight makes it hard to read signs or warnings. Driving uses reflexes so you can quickly react to a problem. Teens have just passed their tests so their reflexes are sharp. Growing up with video games also helps.

The elders drive slower than most probably because they are being cautious but are they too cautious? They may not know it but because they are going slowly the people behind stay close behind them and might not be able to stop in time if the elder stopped short. On the other hand it may be better than some teenagers who aren't cautious at all but their reflexes can make up for most of that. In older years it gets harder to move and by the time you have it could be too late to swerve or turn. Your mind is also slower and doesn't react as quickly.

To some older people driving is something they need. I understand that they like to get around and take care of themselves while they still can. Maybe at 70 people would have to take another test on driving. If they passed their driving test they would next take an eye and reflexes test. If they pass those then they could keep driving. Also, cars could be made that could assist elders in driving.

A young age is better for driving, past 70–75 isn't. Over 75 people shouldn't be driving unless re-tested. I have heard people call younger drivers the ones with the problems yet sometimes it is just the opposite and it's the old ones. The expectancy that if someone does something wrong it must be a teenager is not well thought because it could be just the opposite.

Ms. P: Okay, Rob, you have some interesting reasoning here. You make a pretty good case, and I see you started it off with a question and ended with a solution to the problem. Good job incorporating what we've been discussing in class.

Rob: Thanks.

Ms. P: What I'm noticing at this point is that you have some main ideas here, but you did some overlapping of the ideas in the paragraphs. Do you have your prewrite handy?

Rob: Yes, right here.

Ms. P: Let's take a look. *(I read over the web.)*

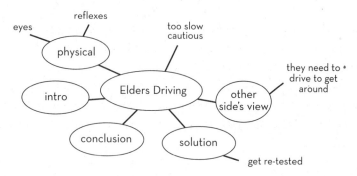

Ms. P: Okay, you have the main ideas here and you stuck to them. Good. What I want you to do, Rob, is go through the paper and see exactly *what* ideas are *where*. I'm going to grab four different highlighters. *(I do, and then hand him the highlighters.)* Leave out the intro and conclusion, and give every other main idea a different color. Do that right now on the prewrite. It doesn't matter what color goes with what idea—just make each idea different.

Rob: Okay. *(He does.)*

Ms. P: Good. Now, go through your draft, this time including the intro and conclusion, and highlight each sentence according to the color you gave it on your prewrite. If it doesn't match anything, then don't highlight it at all. Do you understand?

Rob: I think so . . .

Ms. P: Let's try the first paragraph. The first sentence can be left as it is, but look at your second sentence. What idea does that go with?

Rob: Um, the physical?

Ms. P: Exactly. And you highlighted "Physical" with a blue highlighter, so highlight that whole sentence blue. *(He does.)* Then go to the next sentence. See what I'm asking?

Rob: Oh, yeah, okay. So the whole paper will be covered in different colors?

Ms. P: Right. And if you don't think an idea fits, leave it unhighlighted. Got it?

Rob: Yes.

Ms. P: Okay. I'll check back.

This technique works well when there isn't a lot of deleting to be done, but some rearranging is necessary. As with the scissors technique, the student will have a visual representation of the order of his ideas. Highlighting is also an effective way to see which main ideas, and how much of each, have made it into the introduction and conclusion of an essay.

I see Rob's mistake all the time. In his third paragraph, he stuck with the main idea about "elders" driving too carefully and potentially causing accidents. Then he claimed that the opposite problem—teens driving too carelessly—is also dangerous, but the teens have better reflexes and those reflexes balance out the risk. So far, this harkening back to the first reason does not jumble the organization; in fact, it is a nice bit of layering that gives the essay some cohesiveness. However, what happened next is common among budding writers. His mind was thinking about reflexes again, and when a few new ideas about reflexes surfaced, he added them to the paragraph he was writing that moment. I'm sure he didn't even realize he did it, and I'm hoping that seeing a highlighted block of blue in the middle of a paragraph that should be yellow will alert him.

Another advantage of highlighting ideas is that the student can clearly see the ideas that are unattached to anything in the prewrite. Some unhighlighted sentences will be technical parts of the introduction or conclusion, as in the question Rob uses to open his piece, but others may be new ideas that should either be developed or cut. Highlighting will make this clear. When I return to Rob's desk, I see that he has categorized each sentence and realized there were a few loose ends.

Ms. P: Looks good, Rob—you found a color for almost everything, it seems!

Rob: Yeah. For some I didn't know what to do.

Ms. P: Let's start with what you do know. What do you notice about the essay after doing the highlighting? *(I want him to draw his own conclusions.)*

Rob: Well, some of the paragraphs have two colors in them, and that's probably not good.

Ms. P: That depends. Show me an example.

Rob: In the middle paragraph, it's supposed to be about old people driving too cautiously and the end of it is about reflexes. But it's hard to figure out because this sentence about teenagers is about both. Where should it go?

Ms. P: Excellent question. I think that sentence can stay where it is, because at the core it's about driving carefully, right? You mention reflexes in it, but that's okay—actually, it's kind of a nice touch, because you're reiterating the first reason. You're using your first reason as backup for part of your second reason. You're building on what you've said so far. It's a sophisticated technique, Rob. It holds the essay together as a whole. Good thinking.

Rob: Oh . . . thanks.

Ms. P: The only change I would make to that sentence is to start it by saying, "Some people think it may be better" instead of "On the other hand it may be better." By saying "some people," you separate yourself from that idea, which is the opposite side's view of your topic, right? *(I cross out "On the other hand" and write "Some people think" above it.)*

Clearly, he didn't do it on purpose, but I give him credit as if he did.

Rob: Yes.

Ms. P: So you can acknowledge the other side's view, but you don't want to say it yourself as if you agree on some level. Then the rest of the sentence shoots down that view, in your voice. That's good.

Rob: Okay.

Ms. P: What happens after that sentence, though, is that you go on for a couple sentences about the reflexes. Those sentences don't belong.

Rob: That's what I thought.

Ms. P: Right. You have to find a way to blend them into the first paragraph or cut them if you think they are repetitious or unnecessary. *(I box the sentence group and write "Move up or cut" in the margin beside them.)* Now, where else did you have questions?

Rob: Well, in the second paragraph I saw the same thing—a sentence that could go in two different spots. I have that teens just passed their driving tests, but in the first paragraph, I had driving tests as part of the solution.

Ms. P: I see. Let's look closely at that idea. Does taking a driving test really improve someone's reflexes, or are reflexes something you just have?

Rob: You just have them, but maybe the test lets you practice them.

Ms. P: Maybe, but from what I remember of the driving test, they don't exactly throw things in the middle of the road that you have to swerve around. It's more about testing predictable skills. Nothing unexpected.

Rob: Yeah, I guess you're right. So that idea would be better in the other paragraph?

Ms. P: I think so. It's a strong point in your argument, and I think it would have a bigger impact in the "solution" paragraph. Besides, you're going to be moving some "reflexes" ideas up from the third paragraph anyway, right?

Rob: Oh, yeah.

Ms. P: And you can expand more on the sentence before it. Give an example to illustrate a situation where reflexes are needed. Use sensory details. For example, a dog runs out into the road—what would the driver need to do? What reflexes would he need?

STRATEGY

When giving examples that specifically fit into their essays, I try to use something obvious and then say, "Don't use that, but something like that. You can think of a better example." This technique allows me to illustrate my point while eliminating the obvious, and forces the student to search for something better. In addition, the implication is that the student's yet-unthought-of idea will be something better than what the teacher can think of in that moment. It communicates my confidence in the student and the idea that the student can best determine what the piece needs.

Rob: Oh, okay. (*He writes his own note in the margin: "Put example."*)

Ms. P: Excellent. Don't use that example, but something like that. You can come up with something more interesting with sensory details.

Rob: Okay. Should I keep the video games?

Ms. P: It's an interesting point, and a true one, I think. If you keep it, you should expand on it. Give specific examples. Describe exactly what you mean. Otherwise cut it.

Rob: Okay. (*He writes "Give examples" beside the video games sentence.*)

Ms. P: Here's another spot in the "solutions" paragraph where you should do the same: "they like to get around and take care of themselves." How so? Give some examples. That will make it more vivid to the reader. And I see you left the last sentence in that paragraph blank.

Rob: Yeah. It's a solution, I guess, but it doesn't exactly go with the rest of the paragraph.

Ms. P: You're right about that. You have good instincts for revision, Rob! That's an important skill to have as a writer. Well, you have two choices here. Want to guess what they are?

Rob: Um . . . explain more or cut it?

Ms. P: Right! Now you're getting the idea. You could even make it its own paragraph, kind of a second "solution" paragraph. You'd have to really think of some examples, though, to illustrate what these cars could have. That part could be fun. You could use your imagination.

Rob: Hmm . . . it would be hard to think of how a car could help your eyesight. I'll have to think about it.

Ms. P: Well, it's your choice, Rob. Why don't you work on what we talked about so far, and then we'll take a look at the intro and conclusion, okay?

Rob: All right.

Ms. P: One small change while you're writing: avoid the second person—all these "you's" throughout the paper.

Rob: Oh, right. I forgot.

Ms. P: No problem; just avoid it as you're writing anything new, and later on we'll fix the rest. Do you remember your options?

Rob: Um, use "one" or "someone."

Ms. P: Right, or in your case you could use "a driver." Just keep it in mind.

Rob: Okay.

Later, Rob's revisions look like this:

Young or Old?

I know there is an age to begin driving but should there be an age to end it? At a younger age like 17 eyesight is keen. Your body doesn't have a problem moving the car out of the way fast enough. Teenagers also drive at a steady pace. They just took and passed their driving test so they are aware of the rules required for driving. Older people on the other hand aren't as up-to-date.

As we get older our bodies change again. Our eye sight goes and our reflexes get slower. Driving uses both those skills. Bad eye sight makes it hard to read signs or warnings. Driving uses reflexes so you can quickly react to a problem. In older years it gets harder to move and by the time you have it could be too late to swerve or turn. Your mind is also slower and doesn't react as quickly. For example, if a ball rolls out into the road with a child following it, a driver would have to step on the brake and turn the wheel hard. He or she would have to make sure they didn't hit anyone coming the other way. Younger drivers have faster reflexes to do all of these things. Growing up with video games also helps. Young people practice reacting quickly on the computer for years before they get their licenses. For example, an opponent might jump out from any angle and try to shoot the player. He has to react quickly to save himself. Some video games even have a car that you drive and you have to swerve out of the way of obstacles.

The elders drive slower than most probably because they are being cautious but are they too cautious? They may not know it but because they are going slowly the people behind stay close behind them and might not be able to stop in time if the elder stopped short. Some people think it may be better than some teenagers who aren't cautious at all but their reflexes can make up for most of that.

To some older people driving is something they need. I understand that they like to get around and take care of themselves while they still can. They might have to go to the store, to the doctors, or visit their grandchildren. They don't want to have someone have to drive them everywhere. Maybe at 70 people would have to take another test on driving. That way, the rules of the road would be fresh in their minds, like it is for young people. If they passed their driving test they would next take an eye and reflexes test. If they pass those then they could keep driving.

A young age is better for driving, past 70-75 isn't. Over 75 people shouldn't be driving unless re-tested. I have heard people call younger drivers the ones with the problems yet sometimes it is just the opposite and it's the old ones. The expectancy that if someone does something wrong it must be a teenager is not well thought because it could be just the opposite.

Ms. P: Nice job rearranging, Rob. I see you kept the video games but cut the cars.

Rob: Yeah, it was getting long, and I figured I didn't need the cars.

Ms. P: That's fine. It all fits together well, and you put some more examples in. It's a good revision.

Rob: Thanks.

Ms. P: Let's take a look at your intro from the highlighted draft. Did you notice anything by highlighting each sentence in it?

Rob: Well, the first sentence—the question—didn't fit with any ideas, so I left it blank.

Ms. P: That's alright; it doesn't fit because it's an interesting question that points to your overall thesis. What is your thesis, by the way? Do you see it spelled out anywhere?

Rob: Um . . . I don't see it spelled out in the introduction. It's that older people shouldn't be driving unless they get retested. Here it is, in the conclusion.

Ms. P: Good. Now, as a writer, Rob, you should know right where it is at all times.

Rob: Is it okay in the conclusion? Does it have to be in the introduction?

Ms. P: Well, the reader should know what direction you're headed in from the start. In your case, I think that opening question does point the reader in a certain direction, but the intro as a whole might have more impact if you said something definite as a last sentence of the paragraph. You don't have to use the exact sentence that is in your conclusion, but you should somehow make your opinion clear. *(I write "Thesis?" in the margin next to the intro.)*

Rob: Okay, something like "Old people shouldn't be driving"?

Ms. P: Something like that, but make it a little less blunt—do you know what I mean? Soften it a bit. Use words like "unsafe" or phrases like "some older drivers" or helping verbs like "may" or "might." Don't forget that if an actual audience were to read this, say, in the editorial section of a newspaper, you wouldn't want to offend them.

> *Instead of giving the student a complete sentence, I often offer pieces that could make a thesis and let him decide how to string them together.*

Rob: Oh, right. *(He writes down the suggested words at the top of the page.)*

Ms. P: Now, what about the rest of the intro?

Rob: I have a lot of blue and pink, but not much yellow.

Ms. P: That middle paragraph does seem to be underrepresented in the intro, doesn't it? Can you make it a bit stronger? Maybe just add another clause at the end of the yellow sentence, something that begins with "which . . ."

Rob: Okay. *(He writes "which . . ." above a caret beside "pace.")*

Ms. P: Another revision that will make the whole paragraph flow more smoothly is to add more transition words. I only see one—"also"—and that one gets lost in the middle there. Take a look at the Transition Words poster and throw one or two more in there. Do you think you are adding ideas in the intro or presenting opposite ideas?

Rob: Um, I guess adding.

Ms. P: Right. See on the poster how the transition words for "Adding Ideas" are in blue? On the left side of the poster?

Rob: Yes.

Ms. P: Choose from there. *(I write "Add transitions" in the margin.)* Okay? Work on the intro, and then we just have to clean up the language and you're done. I'll check back.

Again, I'm euphemizing: Rob is going to have to spend some time rooting out the second person and some weak vocabulary. I'd like to have Rob redo his entire conclusion with more specific examples and language, but at this point I'm going to keep him focused on the idea of organization and balance.

CHAPTER 7

Finishing Strong: Conclusions and Clinchers

After a bit of guidance and practice, most students can come up with meaningful introductions. Most students can also get comfortable expressing themes and writing with thematic intention. Writing conclusions and clinchers, though, can be a struggle the whole year through. I find myself telling the students simply, "Conclusions are hard; that's all there is to it. I struggle with them too." It's a weak bit of consolation or encouragement, but it's the truth. What makes conclusions and clinchers so difficult is that they must somehow go beyond simply restating or summarizing. The writer must try to leave the reader with one extra thought, and it should be a meaningful one. Verbalizing the theme can be used quite effectively as an ending technique; however, depending on the specific genre, students may want to try something different. Of course, the theme is the lifeblood to the entire essay. It just need not be stated explicitly in the parting sentence.

In *Teaching Students to Write Effective Essays*, I detail a mini-lesson on ways to end an essay. With each class, I brainstorm a list of what an ideal conclusion should do, and ways it can do it. The students then copy the list into their notebooks for future reference, and I post a class list in the room as well. Throughout the year, we add to this list based on what students discover in the model reading or what they come up with themselves. Of course, certain methods work better with some genres than others; I encourage students to experiment, and as the year progresses, I even mandate that they attempt a technique they haven't yet tried.

FROM "WAYS TO END AN ESSAY"

- Give an opinion.
- Give a brief anecdote that illustrates the main points of the essay, or create a scenario that does the same.
- Pick up where you left off in the introduction, thereby creating a frame for the entire piece.

CLINCHERS

- Give a strong statement of general truth, such as "One must follow his or her conscience."
- Use a sentence with a two-part construction (one independent clause and one dependent clause), like "If . . . then" or "Not only . . . but also."
- Use an image or a simile that can have a symbolic or double meaning.
- Use a sensory detail from earlier in the piece so you end "in the moment."

Many of these techniques can be combined. An effective conclusion for a persuasive essay could give a solution and then use an if/then sentence for a clincher. Not all essays need to end with clinchers, but the final sentence should receive special attention.

For nonautobiographical essays, I like teaching students to try a complex sentence in their conclusions because it compels them to connect two or more facets of the topic. For students who simply repeat their main point over and over, using a sentence with a complex construction encourages them to look at a topic from a new angle. And since this strategy requires only one sentence, it is not intimidating. Students appreciate having sentence constructions suggested to them. It concretizes the task for them. Many times a student will start there and fill in the rest of the conclusion after the two-part clincher is written.

> **STRATEGY**
>
> *Encouraging students to conclude with a complex sentence pushes them to integrate different angles of their topic.*

I don't advocate using questions or statistics in a final sentence. It's not impossible to end an essay with a question or statistic; it's just difficult. Or rather, it's too easy—I fear that if I present those two as options, students will overuse them, asking general, sloppy questions or slapping on a disjointed statistic that would have been more effective earlier in the paper. That said, if a student tries one of these on her own, I wouldn't necessarily stop her. Depending on the class level, my mini-lesson on conclusions and clinchers may even include these techniques, though I caution that they are not as easy as they sound.

AUTOBIOGRAPHY

Using an Image as an Ending

Let's look again at Steve's essay about his go-cart, which appears in full on page 24. After all his hard work, his last sentence fizzles:

> *I got out of my go-cart and I was sweating. I went to my family and they smiled at me and then my dad said, "Your dream came true," and I smiled back. It was the best birthday ever.*

He already stated the theme earlier in the piece, and plot-wise his ending serves to wrap up the scene. It isn't terrible; it just needs a stronger final sentence. I mentally debate if he should simply cut the last sentence, but the penultimate sentence isn't so gripping either. I decide to send him back to his fertile list of details.

Ms. P: Steve, as you know, I think you did a great job with the theme.

Steve: Thanks.

Ms. P: Sometimes, the theme can go right at the end of an essay, and that would be the final sentence or two and serve as a conclusion. But we put yours earlier.

Steve: Right.

Ms. P: So now we have to look again at your last sentence or two and make sure they are as strong as they can be. You have your dad telling you your dream came true and you smiling back at him. That's a nice moment for the ending. Then you say, "It was the best birthday ever." That's the part that's a bit flat. Everyone always says that about their favorite birthday, and your job as a writer is to say something different. Also, can you tell me your verb in that sentence?

Steve: Um . . . "was"?

Ms. P: Right. Do you know what kind of verb "was" is?

Steve: Uhh . . .

Ms. P: Let me give you an example. Right now, in your seat, I want you to start "was-ing."

Steve: What?

Ms. P: Okay, try this: stand up and "was" around the room. *(Steve looks at me, still confused.)* You can't do it, right?

Steve: No.

Ms. P: Right. I'm not trying to make you feel silly, Steve—I'm just trying to show you that the verb "was" has no action. Other verbs do, right? Like "jump," "dance," "write," even "think"—you can do them. What are some others?

Steve: Um . . . "run" or "drive" ?

Ms. P: Exactly. You get it. But "was" doesn't have action. It's called a linking verb. And linking verbs aren't always the best verbs to use in the last sentence of an essay, especially an essay like yours that's so packed with action and details. When you see linking verbs in your writing, especially in the last sentence, treat them like a red flag. Just ask yourself if that's the best way to say that sentence. Maybe it is, but probably not.

Steve: Okay.

Ms. P: I'm thinking you could end with an image—maybe one last vision of the go-cart. That way, the go-cart will be the last picture left in the reader's head. That's what they will think about after they put the paper down. Do you have any details left from the details list?

Steve: I think a few. I definitely didn't use all of them.

Ms. P: Okay. Why don't you skim through it one more time and see if there's something you can use for a final sentence. Like I said, something that would just be one final look at the go-cart as you end the essay.

Steve: I'll try.

If this were another student who did not have the rich list of details that Steve had, I would have the student brainstorm a short list of details that could be developed into an image for the ending. Luckily, Steve finds a wonderful image from his remaining details and inserts it into the last paragraph:

> I got out of my go-cart and I was sweating. I went to my family and they smiled at me and then my dad said, "Your dream came true," and I smiled back. On the way back inside my house I looked back at the go-cart and it was shining back at me.

PERSUASIVE ESSAY

Using Imagery and a Complex Sentence

Here's a conversation with a student who is writing a persuasive letter to the principal of our school about the school's need for new lockers. In the letter, she articulates her thesis and her three reasons: first, that students have to jockey for space, second, that students are consequently late for classes, and third, that students don't have time or space to keep their lockers clean, which results in many lost items. Each reason paragraph has details and examples, and she has an idea for an effective introduction. The final paragraph, however, looks like this:

> I hope you take this letter into consideration. The sooner new lockers are installed in this school, the better. The lockers in our school are old. East definitely needs new lockers to satisfy everyone.

Ms. P: Emily, I told you before how well-organized this letter is, and you use effective reasoning. And it seems that your intro is shaping up nicely too. Good work all around.

Emily: Thanks.

Ms. P: Let's take a look at your conclusion. You reiterate your thesis, but there's not much else there.

Emily: I know. I don't know what else to say.

Ms. P: Conclusions are always difficult; I struggle with them too, all the time. So don't feel discouraged. But let's see what you can try.

Emily: Okay.

Ms. P: How about an image of the lockers? Throughout your paper, you describe the fighting, the tardiness, and the lost items, but we don't yet really have a visual of the locker itself. This might be a good spot for one. Do you think you could brainstorm some details and put them in?

Emily: Yes, I could, since I look at them eight times a day.

Ms. P: Good. Look at this sentence here: "The lockers are old." Instead of just telling us they are old, show us by using description. In your revision, don't use the word "old," but make sure the reader will be *thinking* they are old. Do you understand?

Emily: Yes. Show don't tell.

Ms. P: Exactly. *(I write "Show, don't tell" in the margin and "Use details.")* And see the red flag? You used a linking verb with it. *(I underline "are.")*

Emily: Oh yeah . . .

Ms. P: Then, perhaps you should try an if/then sentence for the very last sentence. Something like "If you really care about . . . then . . ." *(I make a circle with my hands during the pauses to show she must add her own thoughts to the sentence.)*

Emily: Oh, right, yes.

Ms. P: The key is, you have to figure out what your reader *should* really care about. Try this: Look at each of your reason paragraphs again, and see if you could sum up the issue of that paragraph in one word.

Emily: Okay . . . so, the first paragraph, in a word, would be "space"?

Ms. P: Well, go deeper. It's about students not fighting, right? As you say in the letter, "avoiding conflict." *(I'm pushing her to the level of theme.)*

Emily: Oh, so a word would be "peace" or something like that?

Ms. P: Right, exactly—something our principal *should* care about. Now, do the same for the other two paragraphs. *(I write "one meaningful word for each paragraph" and "if/then sentence" in the space after her conclusion.)*

Emily: Okay.

> **STRATEGY**
>
> For a persuasive essay, have the student find one meaningful word to sum up each reason paragraph. Use these three or four loaded words in an if/then construction as the clincher.

When Emily turns in the letter, the conclusion reads:

I hope you take this letter into consideration. The sooner new lockers are installed in this school, the better. The lockers have been dented, scratched, and abused. Some are even falling out of the walls, and many are bolted shut. If you really care about peace, promptness and cleanliness, you will make sure that East gets new lockers for its students.

PERSONAL ESSAY

Revising a Weak Question Into a Strong Statement

Here's an example of what usually happens when students end their papers with a question. After stating the main point a few times, out of desperation they restate it once more as a question, without offering any new insight. Below, Kayla has successfully completed a draft of a personal essay in which she synthesizes opinion, memoir, literary analysis, and research. Although she still needs to work on some spots, for the most part the essay is well-organized and has some examples with potential.

On Friendship

The definition of friendship is "a friendly attachment between persons". I think friendship goes beyond this. Acquaintances can be friendly toward one another. So can strangers passing each other on the street. I think that in order to have a true friendship, trust, honesty and equality must be present. "Friendship is equality" (Pythagoras).

In the fifth grade, one of my friends spread rumors about me around school. Needless to say, that was the end of our friendship. My mother told me that it doesn't matter how many friends you have, as long as you have one or two true friends. "Quality is more important than quantity," she said. This made me feel much better about the situation, because I knew I had at least two true friends. A true friend is someone who you can trust and is always there for you. A true friend never lies to you and respects you. True friendships are extremely important. Everyone needs someone to talk to and needs to be able to trust the person they talk to. Without this quality in life, everyone would be lonely. Francis Bacon once said, "The worst solitude is to have no true friendships."

There are hundreds of books and movies that are based on friendship. The Outsiders by S.E. Hinton is an example of a book based on friendship. In the book, there are two main groups of friends, the socs and the greasers. They formed their friendships as a result of the fact that they were all equal. The socs were all rich, upper class kids and the greasers were all poor. An example of a movie that is about friendship is "The Color of Friendship". The movie takes place during the 1970s when blacks were seriously discriminated against. It is about the friendship that forms between a white girl and a black girl. Although they are often criticized, because their friendship is socially unacceptable, they maintain their friendship through trust, honesty and equality.

Friendship is the most important quality in life. With it comes love, trust, and happiness, three other very important qualities. People bearing no real friendships are at a huge loss. They do not have these three qualities essential to life. What would life be like without friendship?

Ms. P: Kayla, you've done a wonderful job on this so far—you have a lot of ideas on the prewriting sheet, and your essay is well-organized. I can also clearly see your thesis right in the first paragraph. *(I underline the sentence "I think that in order to have a true friendship, trust, honesty and equality must be present.")* Excellent.

Kayla: Thanks.

Ms. P: The part that jumps out at me is the conclusion—it seems like you got a bit stuck there.

Kayla: I did. I didn't know what else to say.

Out of long habit, I try to soften criticism with terms like "somewhat" and "a bit" without pulling back on the work that must be done.

Ms. P: You have one small new idea in the second sentence with "love" and "happiness," but you repeat "trust" in that sentence and call it an "other" quality when it's not an "other"—you've been writing about it throughout your paper. It gets somewhat confusing.

Kayla: Oh, I didn't even realize that. I was trying to summarize I guess. I really didn't know what else to say.

Ms. P: Believe me, Kayla, everyone, and I mean everyone, grapples with conclusions. I certainly do, and so do most adult writers I know. It takes a lot of practice. The fact that you thought of any new ideas at all to put in the conclusion shows you're trying hard and making progress. Many writers struggle to think of anything new beyond what they've already said, so you're ahead of the game.

Lots of eye contact here. The praise is genuine, but I'm also building her up before suggesting that she do more thinking about her examples.

Kayla: Okay.

Ms. P: You also have two great examples with *The Outsiders* and "The Color of Friendship." Those fit your thesis exactly. The first thing I want you to do, though, is go a bit deeper with them. For *The Outsiders*, name characters. And think about the story a bit more—yes, the larger groups were formed because of their socioeconomic similarities. Do you know what I mean by that?

Before she can work on the conclusion, Kayla must strengthen the examples. This will give her more to draw from when constructing the ending.

Kayla: One group was rich and one was poor?

Ms. P: Pretty much. But those weren't the only friendships in the book, were they?

Kayla: No. Cherry and Ponyboy were friends.

Ms. P: Right. Don't you think that friendship was just as important, if not more important in some ways?

Kayla: Yes, but I didn't know how far I should go into the story for this essay.

STRATEGY

Have the student fortify the body of the essay, so there is something meaningful to conclude.

Ms. P: Well, you're right, this essay isn't a book review or story analysis, but to even mention *The Outsiders* without mentioning the friendships that formed outside of the groups kind of misses the major theme of the book, don't you think?

Tone here is important. I want her to be chuckling at herself by the end of the question, not feeling ignorant.

Kayla: Yes, I guess so. *(She is smiling.)*

Ms. P: So ask yourself, what are the qualities of the friendship between Cherry and Ponyboy? Maybe they will be qualities you've already mentioned, maybe they'll have a new twist on what you've already mentioned, or maybe they will be something entirely different. You don't have to make the whole paragraph about them; just name the characters and write a couple sentences about their relationship, and that will do it. *(In the margin, I write "Name characters" and "Explain the crossover friends.")*

Ms. P: Then do the same with"The Color of Friendship." I've never seen that movie—can you tell me a little bit about it right now?

Kayla: This African girl who's white comes to America and lives with an African American family. But it's hard for her—the white girl—because in Africa it was okay to discriminate against blacks but here in America she was living with a wealthy black family. She was really changing because of all her exposure to African Americans. Then her government made her come home.

Ms. P: Wow—that sounds like an interesting movie.

Kayla: It is. I think it was even true.

Ms. P: I'll have to see if I can rent it. Now, after reading your essay, I just assumed the girls were both Americans. If you want to keep that example in the essay, you'll have to explain some of the plot, and make it all its own paragraph. What qualities did the girls' friendship have?

I say "if" she wants to keep the example because she and I both know that the essay is over a page and will remain so even if she cuts this part about the movie, since she will be adding more about The Outsiders. *It's her decision.*

Kayla: Well, the white girl learned that blacks were equal, so their friendship was based on respect and equality. And trust—the white girl learned to trust her black exchange family.

Ms. P: All of that info will help the essay. I think you should keep the example, expand it, and see if it enriches your thesis any more. The thing about a thesis is that even though each example should point directly to it, each example can also deepen it, round it out, show it from different angles. Does that make sense?

Kayla: Yes, I think so.

Ms. P: Okay, let's make some more notes in the margins. Jot down some of what we just said.

Kayla: Okay . . . um . . . *(She writes "Name girls" and "Explain more.")*

Ms. P: Good. Add a phrase like "nature of friendship" or "How are they friends?" so you don't forget the most important part. *(I purposely give her a choice of phrases so she can pick. She writes "nature of friendship" on her paper.)* Do you think you can make those revisions?

Kayla: Yes.

Ms. P: It sounds like you know the answers; you just have to write them. Raise your hand when you're done, and then I'll tell you how we can use the new information to beef up the ending.

Kayla: Okay.

> *Some students naturally write frantically during a conference; some are more passive or simply confused. Often, for the sake of time, I will write my thoughts for them as I speak, figuring I would have done so anyway had the draft been handed in. Kayla seemed to understand my suggestions, so it seems like a good opportunity to help her develop her skills in both note-taking and revising, especially since I had modeled the task when talking about* The Outsiders.

> *"Beef up" is one of my favorite phrases to use during a conference, to the point where the students rib me for it. But it gives the sense that what the student wrote so far is effective and usable. Even in Kayla's essay, where quite a bit of "beefing up" needs to be done, that phrase seems better than saying "totally rewrite" or something more absolute. Of course, there are times when straightforward directives are appropriate too.*

Her revision of the paragraph into two paragraphs appears below:

There are hundreds of books and movies that are based on friendship. The Outsiders by S.E. Hinton is an example. In the book, there are two main groups of friends, the socs and the greasers. They formed their friendships as a result of the fact that they were all economically equal. The socs were all rich, upper class kids and the greasers were all poor. However, even more friendships formed between the groups. For example, Cherry, a soc, befriended Ponyboy, a greaser. Their friendship was not based on equal social status but on respect for each other as people. They trusted each other even though their groups didn't approve. They went outside their groups and found true friendship.

An example of a movie that is about friendship is "The Color of Friendship." The movie takes place during the 1970s when blacks were seriously discriminated against in Africa. A white African girl, Mahree, comes to America as an exchange student and lives with an African American family. This is hard for her since she is used to looking down on blacks in Africa. But she becomes friends with the family's daughter, Piper, and learns that blacks and whites are equal even though they look different and may come from different backgrounds. Their friendship was based on respect for each other and their common interests. (They bonded at the mall shopping for clothes.) Mahree's government disapproves and eventually forces her to leave but Mahree has already learned the true meaning of friendship.

Ms. P: Kayla, this is outstanding! You added in exactly what you needed to. The examples really have some weight now. Great work.

Kayla: Thanks.

Ms. P: Now we're in a good position to work on the conclusion. You have that sentence with "love, trust, and happiness" that doesn't exactly fit, logically speaking. Do you understand why?

Kayla: Because . . . I already talked about trust?

Ms. P: Right. I'm thinking this idea might work well in a "not only . . . but also" sentence. Or even an "although . . . also" sentence with two parts. Look at the poster of transition words. You could even try "while... also." The idea is that you want to repeat your thesis but also add to it. *(I write "not only . . . but also" in the margin beside the sentence.)*

Kayla: Okay.

Ms. P: Looking at your revised examples, is there anything new you can say about friendship? Something beyond trust, honesty, and equality?

Kayla: Um . . .

Ms. P: What's interesting about the friendships between Ponyboy and Cherry, and Mahree and Piper? *(I'm leading her to the words she needs.)*

Kayla: They both had different backgrounds?

Ms. P: Yes, exactly. So true friendship based on trust, equality, and honesty doesn't depend on one's background or race or nationality. *(Now I'm linking her ideas together.)*

Kayla: Oh, okay.

Ms. P: See how you took the thesis a step further with your examples? That is excellent. Jot down "different backgrounds" so you remember that idea.

Kayla: Should I put that somewhere in the conclusion?

Ms. P: Definitely. You've already demonstrated it in your essay, so spell it out in the conclusion. It's a perfect instance of the conclusion summarizing but also having a new twist. It's exactly what I was talking about in the mini-lesson.

Kayla: Okay. Good.

Ms. P: Now, the last part to talk about is your last sentence. You ask a question, but it's a bit general—do you know what I mean by that?

Kayla: Like when we say "in general"? Meaning "overall"?

Ms. P: Right! It means too broad or not specific enough. When I read it, my mind trails off and doesn't have a specific thought or feeling. I can't grasp on to anything. It's the same with the two sentences leading up to it as well. Take a second to read those last three sentences. *(She does.)*

Kayla: Should I just cut them?

Ms. P: Well, you could, but here's another idea: Why don't you try to answer your own question? Have a sentence that describes how life *would* be without friendship. And be specific. Look at those qualities that friendship involves, and think of their specific opposites. For example, what's the opposite of honesty?

Kayla happens to be a student who does exactly what she is asked. Other students may need to be pushed a bit more to round out their examples. In those cases, I would continue to analyze the paragraphs with the student, writing new notes in the margins and sending the student back to work until we arrived at a level of depth appropriate for that student's essay and ability.

Kayla: Dishonesty, lying.

Ms. P: Right. How about trust?

Kayla: Um, not trusting . . . not knowing . . . being afraid?

Ms. P: Good! Fear, right? Now we're getting somewhere. See how words like "lying" and "fear" are so much stronger than terms like "great loss"?

Kayla: Yes. *(She writes them in the margin next to her conclusion.)*

Ms. P: Look at the end of your second paragraph—you talk about being lonely, and you have that great quote by Francis Bacon with the word "solitude." See how that's more specific? *(I point to the second paragraph; she reads. In the margin of the conclusion, I write "Answer question?")*

Kayla: Right. Should I put that quote at the end?

Ms. P: You could, although it does seem to fit right where it is as well. See how your own description goes at the end. You could even try using a simile in the conclusion. *(I add "simile?" in the margin.)* See how it goes and do what you think sounds best. Just be specific.

Kayla: Okay.

I feel confident Kayla will be able to improve the conclusion since she has ample ideas to start with. When she turns in the paper for grading, her conclusion reads:

> *Friendship is the most important quality in life. It not only is a source of trust, equality and honesty, but also a source of happiness and love. Sometimes friendship can be found with people we least expect if we are open to it, it is not based on our backgrounds but our feelings. People bearing no real friendships live with fear, lies and loneliness. They are alone, like a tree in the desert with no water to live on.*

As in Kayla's case, a weak conclusion can point to the weak spots in a student's argument. It is difficult to draw an effective conclusion from undeveloped or disorganized examples. Throughout the year, with each assignment and conference, students learn to see the interrelatedness of all elements in a piece of writing.

CHAPTER 8

Grabbing the Reader: Introductions

In the overall order of conferencing over an essay, working on the introduction comes later. The paper must already have a main idea, details and examples, a theme, and some general organizational scheme. In short, a writer cannot introduce something without knowing what it is she's introducing. So I try to conference with a student about the other main content issues before we discuss how to introduce the piece. If the student comes up with a fitting strategy for an introduction during a conference on another topic, I might have him jot it in the margin or write it out on a separate sheet to return to later, when we are ready.

In *Teaching Students to Write Effective Essays*, I present a mini-lesson on introductions and discuss some strategies for students. Certain strategies work better with certain genres.

FROM "WAYS TO START AN ESSAY"

- Start with a sensory detail.
- Start with the word "imagine."
- Ask a question.
- Give a statement of general truth.

When helping a student form an introduction, I look closely at what already appears in the paper. There's often a suitable detail or a moment with the potential for interesting detail, and we can simply start with that. Or perhaps the essay contains a statistic that can be moved to the beginning in order to attract the reader's attention.

We all tell students not to begin an essay with phrases like "This will be a story about" or "Now I am going to tell about," and students listen. However, most young writers still edge their way into the piece from a distance, using background information which, though helpful, does not exactly make for a gripping beginning.

Starting With a Detail

The next student, Colleen, has done just that: in a story about guiding a woman and her son off thin ice at her local pond, she begins like this:

> I'm a Junior Hockey Patrol, one of the people who tests the ice at our pond, Ice Pond. If the ice is too thin, I must put up the "Danger, Thin Ice" signs. On this particular day, it was windy, but not bitter cold. As I enter the area around the pond, I notice a small boy pushing stacked crates around the ice.

We have already met to discuss the overall structure of the piece and the theme, both of which are in good shape. I feel we can continue with the introduction.

Ms. P: Colleen, as I told you before, this is a wonderful story—you are so brave!

Colleen: Yeah, we get trained for the worst-case scenarios, but you never think you're going to have to use them, you know?

Ms. P: I know. Okay, now, we've met a couple times already, and the story is shaping up nicely. Your theme is clear and you have interesting details throughout. Great job so far.

Colleen: Thanks.

Ms. P: Let's look at your intro. You give us some helpful background information, and I like how you end the paragraph with the conflict—the boy on the ice. However, it's not exactly an attention grabber. I think you need more details.

> *I purposely use the word "conflict," implying that she strategically introduced it where she did.*

Colleen: Okay.

Ms. P: Here's what I'm thinking: can you put us right into the moment of either standing at the pond or approaching the pond? You have a detail here about the wind—"it was windy." That's good to point out, but instead of just telling us it was windy, can you show us? Remember how I'm always saying, "Show, don't tell"? It means—in your case—a writer should give some proof of the wind instead of simply saying, "It was windy," and expecting the reader to believe you based on your word. Do you know what I mean?

Colleen: I think so—I should give an example of wind.

Ms. P: Exactly. Here's a tip-off that you're telling and not showing: you use the verb "was." It's called a linking verb—do you remember this mini-lesson? Linking verbs include "am," "is," "was," "were," "being," "been." They don't have any action. They're like equal signs. That means you're telling. If you use a verb with action, an active verb, you're showing. At any rate, showing the wind might make an interesting introduction. And feel free to add any other sensory details that you can think of. You can give the background information afterward. *(I write "Senses" at the top of her paper as I am speaking.)*

Colleen: Okay. So I should move what I have now to the middle of the paragraph and start with some new sentences?

Ms. P: Exactly. Start in the moment to get the reader's attention, and fill in the background info after. I'll check back.

When I do, she has revised the introduction as follows:

A hair whipped across my face as I began to walk down the hill and across the field to Ice Pond. I don't really know the name of it, but I only go there when it's frozen. The air was still salty from the rain the day before, and the evergreens were a deep, fresh green. I wanted to get there early, to test the ice for thickness. I'm a Junior Hockey Patrol, one of the people who tests the ice, and puts up "Danger, Thin Ice" signs. As I enter the area around the pond, I notice a small boy pushing stacked crates around the ice.

> *True, the third sentence has two linking verbs in it, but I'll let them pass since she does have description in that sentence, and she also used the wonderful "whipped" in the first sentence. In future papers, I'll have her change three linking verbs per paper for practice.*

Ms. P: Wow! The hair is perfect! It puts the reader right there. The salty air and evergreens are nice too. Much better.

Colleen: Thanks!

Ms. P: Okay, I'm thinking that there's a sentence in here that you don't need. Read it again to yourself, and ask yourself: if you had to get rid of one sentence, which one would it be?

Colleen: *(She does.)* Probably the second?

Ms. P: Right. It doesn't really add anything; it only distracts. Unless there is some other special reason you call it that—something that could be meaningful to your story. Is there?

Colleen: No. I just don't know the real name.

Ms. P: And that's all right. "Ice Pond" is the real name for you. Leave it at that, but take out the second sentence. Now, there is one other small revision I want you to make in the intro. Check back in your notebook to the list "Words Instead of 'Walk,'" which we came up with a few weeks ago. Remember that one?

Colleen: Yes.

Ms. P: Good. Pick another verb for your first sentence. It's a perfect spot for a strong "walk" verb, especially since "whipped" is so striking.

Colleen: Oh, yeah, I didn't even realize I used "walk." How about "trek"?

Ms. P: Excellent! Now you don't even need to consult the list. On the next few assignments, I want you to write "strong verbs" and "check for linking verbs" on your Editing/Revising Check Sheet, okay?

Colleen: Sure.

Ms. P: Great work, Colleen. Just print out a fresh copy and hand the whole assignment in. I can't wait to read the whole completed essay!

Colleen: Okay. Thanks!

Starting With a Question

In the following series of conversations, Amy is working on a persuasive essay against the death penalty. Her first sentence is typical of most students' beginnings to a persuasive essay:

> *I disagree with the death penalty. Sometimes, when a person commits a barbaric crime, like murder, for example, they are sentenced to the "death penalty" and are killed themselves by the Justice System, with lethal injections, electrocution, lethal gas, firing squad and even hanging. In the year 1997, 432 people were sentenced to the death penalty by state institutions. Is putting someone to death a just punishment?*

The rest of the paper describes her three reasons for opposing the death penalty: It is hypocritical, it is barbaric in the eyes of the world, and it could kill people who are potentially innocent. We have already worked on the essay's organization and conclusion. For persuasive essay introductions, I don't think students need to have all three of their reasons listed in the introduction, although I don't oppose it either. In Amy's case, I think her list of methods, her statistic, and her tone are enough.

Ms. P: Okay, Amy, let's look at your intro. You use a statistic and a question at the end of it; both are interesting. We also know your position and have some idea where the essay is headed. That's good too.

Amy: Thanks.

Ms. P: My concern is with the first sentence. That's the place where you want to hook the reader, to get them thinking, so that even if they disagree they will keep reading. By putting your opinion right out there, you could lose them.

Amy: Oh.

Ms. P: This is the perfect time to fix it, now that the rest of the essay is in good shape. Most writers save revising the introduction for the end, so you're right on schedule.

Amy: What should I write?

Ms. P: Can you flip your notebook open to the mini-lesson on introductions?

Amy: Okay. *(She does.)*

I'm sensing she is getting discouraged.

Ms. P: Good. Read through the list again, and see if anything jumps out at you. You already have a statistic; if you want, you could simply rearrange the whole paragraph to get that sentence to the top. You have a question also, but I wouldn't put that particular question as the first sentence—it's too open-ended for a very first sentence. You could write something entirely new too. Take a few minutes and think about it; skim through your whole paper and see what would fit best. I'll check back in a few minutes. Okay?

Amy: Okay.

When I come back, her previous first sentence has been replaced with the following:

The U.S. and the death penalty—are they a match?

Ms. P: You decided to start with a new question—good. Tell me more about it. What do you mean, exactly?

Amy: Well, it just doesn't seem right that the U.S. has the death penalty.

Ms. P: How so?

Amy: The U.S. is supposedly the most modern country in the world and we still allow the death penalty. It doesn't make sense.

Ms. P: So you're saying you don't think the death penalty is modern?

Amy: No.

Ms. P: What's a word you would use to describe it?

Amy: Barbaric.

Ms. P: Okay, let's write down everything you just said on the top of your paper. Start with: "The U.S. is supposedly the most modern country." *(She writes.)* Also put "it doesn't make sense" and "barbaric." Now, put it all together to make it your first sentence. You can still phrase it as a question. Start with "Does it make sense that."

Amy: Okay, so it would be: "Does it make sense that the U.S. is supposedly the most modern country in the world and we still allow something as barbaric as the death penalty?"

Ms. P: Right. Get that down. Just rearrange what you already wrote up top.

Amy: Okay. *(She does. I wait.)*

Ms. P: Doesn't that seem more specific? Your old question was a bit confusing for a first sentence, because I as the reader wasn't sure how the two "matched." It seemed foggy. So right from the start I felt a little unsure—that's not how you want the reader to feel after your first sentence. See?

Amy: Right, okay.

Ms. P: Now, let's tighten it up even more. See the linking verb in our new sentence? Circle it.

Amy: Um . . .

Ms. P: Linking verbs include *am, is, was, were, be—*

Amy: Oh! Right here. *Is.*

Ms. P: Good. You want to avoid those when you can. Any ideas how you could get rid of it?

STRATEGY

Like most people, students rarely remember exactly what they just said in a conversation. I scour their thoughts and words for anything they can use. I never say, "Write down what you just said," and walk away. I repeat the phrases and sentences back to the student as I heard them. Sometimes I take notes as a student is speaking so I can give the words back to her accurately.

Amy: Something like "The U.S. has supposedly become the most modern country"?

Students often try to replace one linking verb with another.

Ms. P: Well, you changed the verb, but "become" is actually a linking verb as well. You have to restructure the question a bit. Try using commas: say, "Does it make sense that the U.S.—comma—supposedly the most modern country. . ." See what I'm doing? Try the rest. *(I cross out the verb and write in the first comma.)*

Amy: Okay. "Does it make sense that the U.S., supposedly the most modern country in the world," *(She writes the second comma.)*

Ms. P: Good . . .

Amy: "and we," um . . .

Ms. P: You need to cross out more words.

Amy: "Does it make sense that the U.S., supposedly the most modern country in the world," . . . Oh—"still *allows* something as barbaric as the death penalty." There!

I'm not sure if she believes me or is just agreeing.

Ms. P: Excellent! Doesn't that sound stronger?

Amy: Uh-huh.

> **STRATEGY**
>
> *I always push students to write in as few words as possible, without sacrificing meaning.*

Ms. P: With writing, Amy, usually fewer words are better than more words. If you ever find a place where you can remove some words and still have the same meaning, that's what you should do. Less is more. Does that make sense?

Amy: Yes.

Ms. P: Good. Now the only thing left is to change one of the "barbaric's." You don't want two of them in consecutive sentences. Think about it; use the thesaurus if you get stuck. If you do use the thesaurus, just make sure you choose a word you're already familiar with. Okay?

Amy: Okay.

Amy clearly implies her thesis in her new question; in her conclusion, she reiterates it as a declarative sentence, so I don't think she needs to verbalize it word for word in the introduction. Some other minor changes do need to be made to the paragraph, but to go through each one in a conference would be too time-consuming. Instead, I will make notes on Amy's paper when I grade it; she can make these small revisions herself and ask any specific questions about my notes later.

Starting With a Quotation

In the next conference, Richie needs a strong lead for his piece of historical fiction, which details a snippet in the life of an adolescent Samuel Clemens. So far, his story begins with only facts:

> Sam was a boy of 16 in the year 1851, and a strong one at that. It was truly a regular night in their narrow colonial home in the port city of Hannibal, Missouri. Sam and his younger brother Henry were the only children left at home with their mother, Jane Lampton Clemens. He had a strong build, bushy brown hair and big blue eyes. He also had a scar on his arm.
>
> The three of them sat down to dinner. "How was your day at the printer's, Samuel"? Mrs. Clemens asked.

Ms. P: Richie, as I told you before, this is an absolutely wonderful idea for historical fiction. I can't wait to read the finished product! Did you get all the research you needed to write it?

Richie: Yes, I think so.

Ms. P: Okay, let's look at your lead into the story. You have so many interesting facts in that paragraph: the year, the city, the mom, the home. You also have some interesting details about Twain: his build, hair, and eyes. And alliteration to boot! See what I mean? *(I point to the words.)* All with the letter "b": "build," "bushy," "brown," "big," and "blue." Nice touch!

I'm doing two things here— reinforcing a literary term we've used in class before and acting like he did it on purpose. He might have, but probably not. Still, I don't pass up the opportunity to boost confidence by treating him like a writer who knows what he's doing and who's making deliberate, specific choices about using certain techniques.

Richie: Oh, um, thanks. You know, I didn't do that on purpose.

Ms. P: That doesn't matter. You chose to keep it in instead of revising it, didn't you? Then it's still your choice. It happens to writers all the time—we write something good kind of by accident. We don't know where it came from, but we still decide to use it. Don't you agree?

I'm including him as a writer by using "we."

Richie: Yes. I didn't even know I did it.

Ms. P: That's how it happens! It's still yours. Did Mark Twain really have a scar on his arm?

Richie: I don't know. I put that in myself. It comes in later in the story, remember?

Ms. P: Right! Historical fiction. Good thinking. Okay, let's look at this first paragraph again. You have a lot of important information in here to get the story started, but I think it would be a bit more engaging if you went beyond a list of facts and details.

Richie: Okay . . .

Ms. P: Here's what I want you to do. Wait one minute. *(I retrieve an anthology of short stories from the bookcase in the room.)* Flip through this book—use the table of contents and read the first paragraph of some of the stories. Make a short list in your notebook of methods these writers used to start their stories. I'll check back in a few minutes. Okay?

Richie: Okay. *(When I return, I notice the list on his desk.)*

Ms. P: What'd you find?

Richie: Well, some start right with the action, like they jump into the main action in the story.

Ms. P: Tell me one that did that, for example.

Richie: "The Tell-Tale Heart." In the first sentence he talks about being crazy. And "A & P"—in the first sentence, girls walk into the store in their bikinis.

Ms. P: Good! So we can say the conflict appears in the very first sentence. Right from the start, there is tension. What other techniques did you find?

Richie: Some started with people talking—the quote was the first sentence.

Ms. P: Good.

Richie: Some start with the setting, like this one. *(He points to Eudora Welty's "A Worn Path.")*

Ms. P: Read that one for me.

Richie: "It was December—a bright frozen day in the early morning."

Ms. P: Excellent. So we have some sensory details there, right? A sight and a physical feeling?

Richie: Yes. Most of the stories seemed to fit into one of those categories.

Ms. P: That is excellent, Richie, excellent! Which technique do you think would be best for your story?

Richie: Well, I was thinking that right after my first paragraph the family is sitting down to dinner, so I could have Samuel coming in and getting ready for dinner in the first paragraph. I would make it an action.

Ms. P: That's a wonderful idea. See what details you can pluck out of the original first paragraph and work them in to the scene. For example, instead of saying, "he had bushy brown hair," try to casually get the hair into the action so it seems like a natural part of the scene. Then, whatever details are left you can keep as the second paragraph. Do you remember the character sketch we did last term?

Richie: Yeah.

Ms. P: It's like that. You have all of these nice details about the character, but we can't simply list them—we weave them into a scene where something is happening. Is your character sketch in your permanent folder?

Richie: Yes. I wrote it about my mother.

Ms. P: Good. After we're done, get it and reread it. Then picture that scene with Samuel in your mind. What is Samuel wearing? What

By forcing the reader to notice not only what other writers do, but to categorize these techniques in his or her own words, this lesson reinforces the notion that writing is a craft and not some divine inspiration bestowed on a select few. The student isn't a passive receiver of knowledge in this exercise; he is a sleuth in pursuit of a missing puzzle piece. In some classes, I do this as a whole-class mini-lesson and we compile a list as a group.

I constantly refer to past writing assignments. I want the students to understand that the skills they learn with each piece have continued relevance in subsequent writing.

does the room look like? What is Samuel doing? *(I write down "Clothes?" "Room?" and "Action?" at the top of his draft.)*

Ms. P: Let me give you something else to think about. *I point to his first paragraph again.)* See where you say he is "strong" in the first sentence, and later in the paragraph you say he has a "strong build"?

Richie: Oh, right, yes.

Ms. P: You really only need to say that once. And what would be even better is if you could *show* us he is strong instead of, or in addition to, just telling us. In writing, we always say, "Show, don't tell." It means that the writer shouldn't take the easy way out by saying things like "He was strong" or "It was cold" or "The dog was angry." You have to show us muscles or ice or growling teeth. Do you understand?

Richie: Yes, yes, I think so.

Ms. P: Try this: In that paragraph, don't even use the word "strong," but make it so I will think to myself, "Wow, he's strong," when I read it.

Richie: Okay.

Ms. P: Actually, Mark Twain himself has one of the most famous quotes around about showing and not telling. It goes: "Don't say the old lady screamed. Bring her on and let her scream."

Richie: He really said that?

Ms. P: Yes! Isn't it funny that he's giving you advice from the grave about how to write a story about him?

Richie: Yes, it's ironic that I'm writing the paper on him and he said it. *(I write down the quote at the top of his open notebook page.)*

Ms. P: I'm sure you know that Mark Twain has dozens of famous quotations that are easy to look up. You know what would be clever? If you read some and worked one in to your story somewhere.

Richie: Yeah—like he said it as a kid.

Ms. P: Right! You'd have to find one that fits; you couldn't force it in. Try the quotation dictionary on the shelf; look up "Mark Twain" in the index. Then look online.

Richie: That would be good if I could find one.

Ms. P: For now, work on the intro and see what you can do with Samuel's "strength." I'll check back.

I write down "Use actual Twain quote?" at the bottom of his draft. There's a fine line between giving a student an idea that he can mold into his own and writing the story for him. But I seize any opportunity to rejuvenate the student's interest in the piece; here, Richie is actually excited to go leafing through a classroom reference book.

When I return to Richie's desk, his new introduction read as follows:

"Here's the firewood you wanted, Mother." Samuel Clemens came in to the house carrying a large load of wood wrapped in a log carrier. His square shoulders made it look easy. He set it down beside the stone fireplace in the main room and put two logs onto the dying fire. Sam adjusted his wide-rimmed glasses and brushed dust off his

blue button-down shirt and black pants. His bushy, brown hair covered up his big, blue eyes. The scar on his arm showed as he also put away the paper and pencils he always carried on him, accept for dinner.

Sam was a boy of 16 in the year 1851. It was truly a regular night in their narrow colonial home in the port city of Hannibal, Missouri. Sam and his younger brother Henry were the only children left at home with their mother, Jane Lampton Clemens.

The three of them sat down to dinner. "How was your day at the printer's, Samuel?" Mrs. Clemens asked.

Ms. P: Richie, this is excellent! I see you decided to use a quote as the opening line.

Richie: Yes, it seemed the easiest way to start the action.

Ms. P: You did a great job showing he is strong, you worked in all the details about his appearance, and you even added something new—the paper and pencils. I love it!

Richie: Thanks.

Ms. P: You really pulled it off. Look at the two drafts. *(I arrange them side by side.)* See how it is so much more interesting to dive right into the scene than to list the background information? Even the bushy hair feels more vivid because it is part of the action.

Richie: Yes. Uh-huh.

Ms. P: Okay, while it's fresh in your mind, let's strengthen one spot and then you can hand it in.

Richie: Okay.

Ms. P: Look at your verb in the second sentence. What is it?

Richie: *Came in?*

> *I'm always tentative about pushing kids after they've already done a good bit of work on one aspect of the piece. At the same time, I want students to be in the habit of constantly strengthening their language. I feel like Richie can handle it.*

Ms. P: Right. You could easily use a stronger word or words. Ask yourself, how did he come in? Did he rush in or burst in? Did he slip in? Did he saunter in? See how the choice of word there will affect the whole paragraph?

Richie: Yes, yes. *(He writes down some of my examples.)*

Ms. P: See if you can replace that verb, and then you're ready to hand everything in. Always be on the lookout for places you can be more exact, especially with verbs.

Richie: Okay.

Ms. P: Excellent work, Richie. I can't wait to read the whole story with all the revisions!

Richie: Thanks.

I resist asking him to put an adjective before the log carrier or giving him a refresher course in punctuating quotations. The latter I will write on the paper when I grade it; the former I will let go. I could also go through his entire paper with a fine-tooth comb for weak verbs, but I won't. Focusing on the part that we have labored over is most meaningful and effective. When I grade his paper, I may circle one or two more weak verbs to reinforce the lesson, but that's all.

Starting With a General Statement of Truth

In the next conversation, Eileen is writing an analysis of Ray Bradbury's "All Summer in a Day." She understands the purpose of an introduction and has written several successful intros for previous assignments. When I stop by her desk, she is reading a draft of her paper, which still lacks a beginning.

Ms. P: How's it going, Eileen?

Eileen: Good, I'm just trying to figure out the introduction.

Ms. P: Let's see what you have so far . . . a thorough plot summary—good; paragraphs on conflict and symbolism—excellent. You really understood this story well, Eileen.

Eileen: Thanks. Even though it's about living on Venus, it seems like it could happen anywhere.

Ms. P: I know. The themes can be true for anyone. That's what makes it such an engaging story. Actually, I see you wrote a lot about the theme in your draft and here in your prewrite.

Eileen: Yeah. I can just imagine what it's like to be treated badly for being different.

Ms. P: What are you thinking for the introduction?

Eileen: I don't know. I looked at the list of how to do an intro, and nothing's jumping out at me.

Ms. P: Did you flip through the sample book reviews?

Eileen: Yes, and I reread the sample essays from the assignment folder.

Ms. P: Good. Well, you have enough information in the essay that you really can't go wrong. You could use a quote from the story, you could ask a question, you could re-create a scene from the story, using details. Actually, since you already wrote a lot about the theme of the story, you could start with that, in the form of a general statement.

Eileen: Yeah, I thought about that too.

Ms. P: How about this: narrow it down to two techniques, and try both of them. Save two versions of your essay, one for each technique. Then we can look at both and see which is better. Even if you're not sure about what you're writing, just write anything so we can compare it and have a place to start. How does that sound?

Eileen: Good.

Ms. P: Can you choose two? You can try three if you want.

> Voices From the Middle *is a journal that includes book reviews in each issue. They are detachable, index-card-sized, and printed on cardstock, and I collect and keep them in an index-card box on a shelf in my classroom library. I often send students to the box to read the introductions there for ideas. These sample introductions usually fall into one of the categories in "Ways to Start an Essay," which the students have in their notebooks, but it is always helpful to see the techniques in action.*

> *This technique is effective on many levels. First, it gives the student something to do and breaks through the block. Even though Eileen is a confident writer and usually gets assignments done quickly, like the rest of us, she sometimes gets caught up in the small choices, which can lead to indecision and frustration. Forcing oneself to write anything, even something "bad," can help in getting out of that cycle. It will also allow Eileen to compare two introductory approaches and analyze their effectiveness. This is a high-level practice that will help her make good choices in future essays.*

Eileen: No, I'll do the theme and maybe . . . the "imagine" opening.

Ms. P: Good. Raise your hand if you have any problems. Show them to me when you're done.

The next day, Eileen approaches my desk with the two introductions:

1. *Imagine not seeing the sun in seven years. It rains every day and only once in seven years does the sun come out. Then imagine if you waited all that time to see the sun, and someone prevented you from seeing it. You would have to wait another seven years.*

   In this story, the main character, Margot, is an Earth girl who had moved to Venus when she was four.

2. *When people are with others that are just like them, it is easier to get along with them. But, when a new different type of person is introduced, they are treated as an inequality, and often left out. When this happens, people should look beyond differences, and find similarities, and get along as best they can.*

   In this story, the main character, Margot, is an Earth girl who had moved to Venus when she was four.

Ms. P: Good work, Eileen. What do you think?

Eileen: Well, I like them both, but the first one seems kind of boring. And I describe it all again in the second paragraph anyway.

Ms. P: If you wanted to use the first one, you would have to add some specific details so that the reader *could* imagine it—right now it's hard to imagine, since we always see the sun. You would have to make it more vivid.

Eileen: I think I like the second.

Ms. P: You know what I like about it? In it, you talk about the theme in general terms. Then in the last paragraph of your essay you talk about it specific to Margot and her classmates. It makes a frame for the entire piece. That's a sophisticated technique. Really polished. Good thinking.

Eileen: Thanks.

Ms. P: Now, there are just a couple small things you have to do to blend it in to the rest of the piece. First, you should mention the title and author at the end of the paragraph, along with your main idea. The intro should always contain a specific idea—a thesis— that tells us where the rest of the piece is headed. *(I write "thesis?" in the margin of her draft.)*

Eileen: Oh, yeah. Okay.

Ms. P: Then, the only place I'm stumbling when I read it is over the word "inequality." That term is used more for a thing than a person. You could get away with it, but why use a word that would distract the reader? As a writer, you want the reader to be focused on your message, not wondering if you used a word correctly or not. See if you can smooth it over.

> *This seems like a small concern, but I'm not nitpicking. I want students to learn to feel the texture of words and to truly deliberate over word choice. Of course, as a writer myself, I enjoy this struggle. I try to communicate that too.*

Eileen: Okay. How about just "they are treated unequally"?

Ms. P: Excellent. Saying the same thing in fewer words is always better. Good job.

Eileen hands in her paper with these changes. I will help her revise the small grammatical glitches throughout the paper when I grade it.

As mentioned previously, I say this often. I omit the second truth: that using fewer words is always harder. If this is the only style rule they remember, I will have succeeded.

> *When people are with others that are just like them, it is easier to get along with them. But, when a new different type of person is introduced, they are treated unequally, and often left out. When this happens, people should look beyond differences, and find similarities, and get along as best they can. This, I think, is the main message in Ray Bradbury's "All Summer in a Day."*
>
> *In this story, the main character, Margot, is an Earth girl who had moved to Venus when she was four.*

AUTOBIOGRAPHY

Using Sensory Detail and Flashback

One of the easiest ways to rev up the introduction of a narrative is to break the piece in half, start with the most compelling moment of sensory detail, include the rest as a flashback, and unite the whole piece at the end.

After we finished conferencing over her theme, I talked to Lauren one more time about her introduction. The final version of her paper can be found on page 77, but here are the first few sentences:

Most students can easily rearrange their essays to begin in medias res.

> *My dad had decided to take my brother and I on a canoe ride to see the fireworks. We had to park the car in front of someone else's house, and ask their permission to go into the water from their backyard. They said yes, but were reluctant to let us do so, since it was almost dark.*

Ms. P: Okay, Lauren, what we're going to do now is a bit of rearranging. The first few sentences of the piece start by giving us some background and then telling us step by step what happened. I think it would be stronger if you put us right in the moment, right in the middle of things. No lead-ins. Just put us right there, on the lake.

Lauren: Okay . . .

Ms. P: The good news is, you don't have to write anything new. We can take details you already have and move them up to the top. That way, the first paragraph will put us right in the middle of the action, and we'll keep that background information and step-by-step narration for the *second* paragraph. By then, the reader will be hooked, and once you have them hooked, you can backtrack and fill in the background info. Does that make sense?

Lauren: Yes.

Ms. P: It will be a flashback. Do you know what I mean by that?

Lauren: Yeah. The story goes back to something in the past.

I'm constantly trying to convince students that they can use the literary techniques they learn in English class. They don't have to be professional writers, and they don't have to produce "good" writing by accident. They can, and should, craft their writing with a purpose.

Ms. P: Exactly. Can you think of any movies or books that use a flashback at some point?

Lauren: Um . . . maybe like in *Titanic*, when the main character is older and tells the story from memory?

Ms. P: Right! It's a sophisticated technique, and you have all the details here to do it. Now, where in your story is the most interesting spot to begin?

Lauren: Probably . . . sitting on the lake watching the fireworks.

Ms. P: That's what I was thinking too! Except maybe start right *before* the fireworks begin—just sitting on the lake and waiting. That way there's a moment of suspense, where the reader is wondering what will happen to you in the canoe on the lake.

I often ask a student a question and excitedly tell her that I was thinking the same thing. I may revise the thought from there, but the point is to reward and encourage the student for having any answer at all instead of just saying "I don't know."

Ms. P: Skim through and pull out some interesting in-the-moment-on-the-lake details. Can you find them?

Lauren: Um . . . *(She looks.)* Here. The part about the bugs on the water.

Ms. P: Excellent. Those three sentences are wonderful details. Let's move them to the beginning. *(I circle the sentences and draw an arrow to the top.)* Make them their own paragraph, and make your current first paragraph the second paragraph. That will be an interesting introduction, don't you think?

Lauren: Yes. In the moment. I get it.

Ms. P: Just to make it clear, you could use a phrase like "earlier that day" when you flash back into the past from sitting on the water. That way we'll know for sure you're going further back into the past.

Lauren: Okay. *(She writes the phrase next to the appropriate paragraph.)*

Ms. P: Alright. Let me point out one more spot and then you can revise the intro and hand it in. Look at that first sentence about your dad: "My dad had decided to take my brother and *I*"—there's a problem there, with the grammar.

Lauren: Really?

Ms. P: Yes. It's with "my brother and I."

Lauren: I thought we were always supposed to say "I" and not "me and my brother."

Ms. P: Well, almost. You're right that the other person should come first. But we use "I" when it's the subject, usually coming in the beginning of the sentence. In your sentence, that word is an object, meaning it receives the verb.

Lauren: How do I know which to use?

Ms. P: Here's an easy way to test it: In your mind, remove the other person from the sentence—in this case it would be your brother. Then read it. Do that now.

Lauren: Um . . . "My dad had decided to take . . . I"?

Ms. P: Yes. Does that sound right to you?

Lauren: No.

Ms. P: Right. What would you say?

Lauren: "My dad had decided to take *me*."

Ms. P: Exactly. If that's what you would say with just yourself in the sentence, that's what you should say with someone else added in there too.

Lauren: Okay.

Ms. P: You do it again later on. Look at this sentence: "My dad reassured my brother and I." Do the same test on it.

Lauren: "My dad reassured" . . . it should be "me." *(She writes in the correction.)*

Ms. P: Right. You got it. It's a small point, but one to remember. Now just move those sentences up top for the intro, and you're done. Great work.

Lauren: Thanks.

The fact that she did it twice is what prompted me to explain it to her. Otherwise, I would have just circled the single mistake when I graded it.

In the end, Lauren's paper looks like this:

As I stared at the water, I could see small bugs darting to and fro across the surface. There was a cool breeze blowing, but I didn't feel cold. We drifted for a while silently, hearing the sounds of voices from parties along the shores.

Earlier that day, my dad had decided to take my brother and me on a canoe ride to see the fireworks. We had to park the car in front of someone else's house, and ask their permission to go into the water from their backyard. They said yes, but were reluctant to let us do so, since it was almost dark. My dad and brother had to carry the canoe, so all I had to do was hold the flashlight on their path. I was glad about that because I wouldn't want to be carrying a canoe in the dark. We had to step over a wire to get into the water, and then step onto a small rickety bridge, which was only big enough to hold one person at a time. Then, we started to paddle out into the middle of the lake. Actually, I didn't have to paddle the canoe, so I just stared up at the night sky, waiting for the fireworks to begin.

I wasn't in a great mood. I didn't feel like saying anything because I had argued with my dad earlier that day about going out with my friends. I had wanted to go watch the fireworks with my Kristen and Amy, but my dad insisted that my brother and me go with him. I didn't like how he treats me like I'm still a child like my brother.

My dad reassured my brother and me that this was a good view, but we were skeptic. All of a sudden, we heard cheering from the shores, where families were having parties. The fireworks had started, and my dad had been right. We had the best view in the town. Everywhere you looked in the sky, there were fireworks of all shapes and sizes. There were sparkles, shimmers, explosions, squiggly lines and even smiley faces. We saw every firework twice—once in the sky and once in the water. I realized then that my dad had planned this nice surprise for me and my brother, and he just wanted to share it with us.

On the shores all around us, people were setting off their own firecrackers, competing to see who had the most, and whose "show" was better. They were extremely loud and very brightly colored. The crackling of the firecrackers and beauty of the fireworks was stunning. The experience I had was wonderful. As the finale came to an end, I leaned over toward my dad and saw the lights flashing on his face. I even saw tiny fireworks reflected in his eyes. He looked at me, smiling, and I said, "Thanks."

> *Pushing every paper to perfection during conferencing only saps the student's energy. Having a few days' break from the piece gives the student fresh eyes; often, she will revise or strengthen the draft above and beyond my suggestions, once she has had a chance to sleep on it.*

Lauren does have a bit more to polish in the piece, but she can do that on her own. I don't have the time to conference over every small revision that every piece needs; additionally, students need a break from me and the intensity of the conferencing. From the beginning of the year, I train them, in mini-lessons and early conferences, to know how to fix minor issues in grammar and language themselves. Lauren includes a few weak words she should change, like "good" and "great"; I will also circle "step over" and "step onto" in the second paragraph and write "Replace one" in the margins. I might even write "Use onomatopoeia here" at the end of her new introduction, to describe the voices of the shoreline partiers. For now, though, I think Lauren has absorbed as much as she can.

AUTOBIOGRAPHY

Using Sensory Detail and Flashback

The in medias res method also works well with Steve, the student first seen in Chapter 4. After Steve makes a final revision to his conclusion, I meet with him one more time to talk about his lead. So far, it reads:

The Perfect Day

Early that morning my uncle called me on the phone and told me that he was going to bring some magazine's for my birthday. Around twelve I was eating my birthday cake and I herd a sound and the sound sounded like a lawn mower getting started. I did not pay attention to it and my friend came running to the door and yelled "There is a go-cart outside and it is with your uncle." I did not believe him so I went outside and saw it and I was speechless. My family yelled, "Happy Birthday!" That by far was the best birthday gift.

The go-cart had dark green bars and a leather seat. It was a humid day in the summertime and I hoped in. I held on to the leather-wrapped steering wheel. I could smell the exhaust. I revved up the engine like a chainsaw and slowly backed up. My mom was clapping and jumping a little bit.

I backed into the street and for a second their was silence and birds chirping. And then I switched gears and stepped on the gas and broke that same silence. The wheels started to spin and it sounded like a car peeling out on a rocky driveway.

I was having a blast on my new go-cart. I was going as fast as I dreamed. I saw mailboxes and cars lined up on the street that I never noticed before. It was like going threw a tunnel. I was in a new world. Neighbors waved. The only down side of the day was the street I had been riding on was very bumpy and I was hitting my head every minute.

I came to a stop sign and stopped. I noticed the yellow lines on the street and black gravel. The purr of the engine was like a kitten.

I stepped on the gas and the wind was blowing on my cheeks. I was going so fast it felt like I was in the air flying away. I saw new streets I did not know were there. I felt like I was in my own world. It was like riding in a time capsule.

Riding the go-cart made me feel free, like I had my own space. Everything felt far away, like school, homework, money worries, and my sister. I realized my parents knew how hard I was working at school and were proud of me.

I got out of my go-cart and I was sweating. I went to my family and they smiled at me and then my dad said, "Your dream came true," and I smiled back. On the way back inside my house I looked back at the go-cart and it was shining back at me.

Ms. P: All right, Steve, we're in the home stretch. I'm just amazed at how far this piece has come. You've been working hard and it shows.

Steve: Thanks.

Ms. P: The last aspect to focus on is the beginning of the story. Do you remember what a writer needs to do in the first paragraph of any story or essay?

Steve: Um . . . not really. Describe something?

Ms. P: Well, think of it this way: what subject do you find least interesting?

Steve: Social studies.

Ms. P: Okay. If you picked up a book and it started with the date of Benjamin Franklin's birth and where he went to school and who his parents were, would you be interested?

Steve: No.

Ms. P: But what if you opened that book and it started with a man standing out in a crashing storm, rain pummeling him, and he was struggling to hold on to the string of a kite that was whipping around in the sky above him. Lightning was flashing all around, and he was waiting, hoping that some would crack near him. Would you read to see what happened?

Steve: Maybe, just to see if he got hit or not.

Ms. P: Right. It's the same guy—Ben Franklin—but it all depends on how the story starts. So do you see the importance of the introduction?

Most students learn this in the early grades.

Steve: Oh, right, to get the person's attention.

Ms. P: Right. Now let's look at what you have so far. Your uncle called you and he was going to bring some magazines. Then you jump ahead a few hours to you eating birthday cake. Do you think that would grab the reader's attention?

Steve: Not really.

Ms. P: Me neither. But I'll tell you an easy way to change it. You already thought of all those wonderful details, right?

Steve: Yeah.

Ms. P: Well, I think we can use what you have—we're just going to move things around. Skim through and tell me where you think the most interesting details are in the story.

Steve: Okay, well, the lawn mower . . . um . . . peeling out . . . going fast . . . wind on my cheeks.

Ms. P: Good. I agree, those are all interesting. What if we took one of those, like the wind on your cheeks, and used that as the beginning? We'll start right in the middle of the action, in order to get the reader's attention, and then we'll backtrack to the rest of the story. How does that sound?

> I already pegged that "wind" paragraph as a good place to start, but I want him to feel like he's in control. He could start with any of the details he mentioned, and I will give him that option too.

Steve: Good.

Ms. P: Do you see any other spots that would make a better beginning? Or do you want to try another detail that you mentioned, like the lawn mower sound? You could try anything.

Steve: No, I like the wind.

Ms. P: Me too. It has the added bonus of touching upon the theme at the end of that paragraph—the "in my own space" idea. That way, the reader gets a taste of it right from the beginning. So, what you want to do is just cut and paste that paragraph to the top, and we'll see how it looks. Do that now, and print a fresh copy, and I'll check back in a minute.

> I don't want to go any further with this until Steve can see the paragraph at the top. It gives me a quick minute to check in on someone else. When I notice Steve at his desk with the new version, I return.

Steve: Okay.

Ms. P: Let's see what it looks like. Good. I think it sounds great that way, don't you?

I stepped on the gas and the wind was blowing on my cheeks. I was going so fast it felt like I was in the air flying away. I saw new streets I did not know were there. I felt like I was in my own world. It was like riding in a time capsule.

Early that morning my uncle called me on the phone and told me that he was going to bring some magazine's for my birthday. Around twelve I was eating my birthday cake and I herd a sound and the sound sounded like a lawn mower getting started. I did not pay attention to it and my friend came running to the door and yelled "There is a go-cart outside and it is with your uncle." I did not believe him so I went outside and saw it and I was speechless. My family yelled, "Happy Birthday!" That by far was the best birthday gift.

Steve: Yeah. It's right in the action.

Ms. P: Exactly. But we do have to change one more thing—the verb in the sentence when your uncle called. Right now it sounds like your uncle called while you were in the middle of riding the go-cart. That's because everything is in the simple past tense—the regular past tense. Read it to yourself quietly right now. Isn't it a bit confusing? *(He reads.)*

Steve: I guess so.

Ms. P: You need a *double* past tense, to show that something happened before the rest of the story, which is in the regular past tense. It's called the past perfect tense. It's easy to do—just use "had" with the verb. What's the verb—the action—in that first sentence?

Steve: Um . . . *bring?*

Ms. P: That's an action, but not the one I was looking for. That one can actually stay the way it is because it has the word "to" before it. Look in the first part of the sentence.

Steve: Oh—*call.*

Ms. P: Right. Now, put *had* in front of it.

Steve: *Had called?*

Ms. P: Exactly. That shows that it happened before the go-cart ride.

Steve: Okay.

Ms. P: And that's it! It's ready to be handed in. Steve, you really did an excellent job on this. Look at your first draft. *(He shuffles through the drafts and finds it.)* You went from this—to this. That took a lot of work and thought.

Steve: I know!

Ms. P: But look how great it is—you have so many interesting details, a deeper meaning, and an attention-grabbing intro. It's a wonderful piece of writing. You should feel really proud.

Steve: Yeah, it took a long time. This is the longest thing I ever wrote.

Ms. P: Good! And doesn't everything take a long time if it's worth it? Writing is just like a sport or anything else you want to be good at—you have to keep working on it. Great job, Steve.

Steve: Thanks.

When I'm grading his paper, I will circle the misspelled homophones and the other grammar mistakes. I squeezed in the past perfect because it was such a relevant point and teachable moment. Other than that, though, Steve has done all he can do. I invested a lot of time with him in this early assignment, in the hope that he will remember the importance of having an introduction and theme in subsequent assignments. Many students do not need as much guidance as Steve—they get the big concepts during the mini-lessons and require only gentle reminding at times. Students like Steve need more help, but completing each task and turning out a successful final piece builds their confidence as writers.

CHAPTER 9

Using the Best Words

When I first evaluate a piece of student writing, I make sure the essay has all the necessary parts to make it an essay (details, theme, conclusion, introduction) and that those parts are in a comprehensible order. From there, I help the student revise the language. However, as the conversations in the book indicate, the writing and revision process is circular. In order to craft an introduction, students must write some details. As they write, I steer them away from linking verbs. I do not resist nudging students along in language as I help them find a theme or a thesis or an entirely new structure for the essay. This is because writing, the act of putting one's thoughts in words, often *creates* new thoughts. We sit down at the page with some ideas, maybe even with a detailed outline, or maybe with a few definite phrases or whole sentences or even a paragraph written in our heads, but we always create more in the moment. The words we choose in that moment of creation shape the new thought and set the tone for the next thought. Thus, although I never aim to overwhelm a student—no one writes perfectly in a first draft, and the pressure to do so will stifle ideas—I nevertheless try to plant the seeds in students of habitually strengthening language *as they write*. Strengthening one's language at the moment it is formed strengthens the quality of our thoughts. If students can form the habit of not just writing in strong language, but *thinking* in strong language, their writing reaches an entirely new level even before the pen hits the page.

> The act of writing not only records thoughts but creates them.

I do acknowledge that strengthening language as thoughts emerge is difficult to do and almost impossible to measure (though that does not diminish my belief in the benefit of the effort). During conferences, I do not nitpick every instance of weak language. Rather, at some point in the series of conferences for an assignment, I will make a suggestion focusing on one aspect of language. It may be at the end, or the opportune moment may present itself earlier. This communicates to the student that although in class we discuss discrete aspects of the writing process, it does not happen that way in the mind.

The most effective way to instill the habit of strong thinking is to give students guidelines for thinking before they even begin to brainstorm for a piece. I do this in a variety of ways. First, early on in the year, I ban certain words from the class. I'm not referring to the usual four-letter words (although it goes without saying these are prohibited); I'm talking about other, almost-as-offensive four letter words like *good*, *cool*, and *nice*, as well as their shorter or longer relatives: *bad, great, awesome, stuff, things,* and sometimes *items* or *excellent*.

I post signs around the room with these words in the middle of a red circle with a slash through it, and I explain to students why the words are banned and how to push themselves to use more meaningful, more specific language. I tell them that after my class, they can return to using those words if they wish; it is my hope that the habit will instill itself by the end of the year and that for the rest of their lives they will think twice before using them in their writing. Students lose points on my rubric for using banned words (although they are free to revise a paper as many times as they wish). I explain that the words themselves aren't evil, just empty. We all use them when speaking (including me), and most writers (including me) even use them when writing. It is possible for these words to be used effectively. Middle school students, however, use them not to accomplish a specific purpose but out of mindless habit and shallow thought. Students who use such words are not immoral or inherently lazy; they are just untrained and have not been challenged to consistently think harder about words. My goal is to devote just one of their formative years to forcing them to push their minds. It's like boot camp: a person won't choose to live that way forever, but the lessons learned during that time can be used when needed—or even unconsciously if the habits become strong enough.

BANNED WORDS

good
bad
nice
great
awesome
cool
things
stuff

Shortly after the mini-lesson on banned words, I conduct a similar mini-lesson on banned clichés. For most students, this mini-lesson is their introduction to the concept and why clichés should be avoided.

The second major way I try to cultivate vibrant thought and language is by showing students how to summon sensory details. A lesson or two after the introduction to banned words, I lead students through a mini-lesson on sensory details, and for the rest of the year, regardless of the genre we are studying, I refer students back to that lesson and have them make lists. I include a sensory details section on most prewriting sheets. As with avoiding banned words, I try to make using sensory detail a habit of students. By anchoring writing in a specific moment, the writer avoids the generalizations that are the hallmark of weak language.

Another general rule I teach is to avoid beginning two sentences the same way in one paragraph. This curbs the repetitive "It is" and "There are" structures. I introduce the broader principle "Vary your sentence structure" as well, but presenting it as a simple rule gives the students a specific guideline. I post this maxim on a wall in the room. If a student has too much repetition elsewhere in his sentences, I deal with that in an individual conference.

STRONG LANGUAGE MINI-LESSONS

☐ Banned Words

☐ Clichés

☐ Transition Words

☐ Second Person Pronouns

- ☐ Sensory Details
- ☐ Sentence Variation
- ☐ Linking Verbs
- ☐ Passive Voice

- ☐ Verb-Preposition Combos
- ☐ Verbs Instead of "Said"
- ☐ Using a Thesaurus

When appropriate, I deal with the overuse of linking verbs and the passive voice in individual conferences but I also conduct mini-lessons on these topics about midyear. Changing sentence structure in order to incorporate a better verb requires abstract thought and can be intimidating. Although I believe the mini-lessons help some students, more is achieved during a conference when I can walk students through reshaping their own sentences.

Throughout the year I teach other mini-lessons on how to strengthen verbs. In one lesson, we work on changing a verb-preposition combination into a single-word verb. In another, I have each class generate a long list called "Verbs Instead of 'Said'" and we post a cumulative list from all the classes for reference. Later, we come up with the list "Verbs Instead of 'Walk.'" We also have mini-lessons on employing a variety of transition words, and on how and when to use a thesaurus. By constantly practicing with students how to come up with more interesting word choices, I model how effective writing gets done.

Because I teach strong language to the whole class throughout the year, the students know it is a priority for all assignments, and that I expect each student to put effort into the language he uses, and that I'm not just being picky during individual conferences.

PERSUASIVE ESSAY

Replacing Banned Words

Weak language still appears in students' papers. They're beginners after all, and instilling new habits takes time. During conferences, I try to be as supportive as possible, always assuming (unless I definitively know otherwise) that the student is trying her hardest. Let's look again at an essay from Chapter 6 (see page 51). We last left Rob working on changing all the second-person references to the third person. When I visit him again, I notice a few spots that need work in his second paragraph, which reads as follows:

> As we get older our bodies change again. Our eye sight goes and our reflexes get slower. Driving uses both those skills. Bad eye sight makes it hard to read signs or warnings. Driving uses reflexes so the driver can quickly react to a problem. In older years it gets harder to move and by the time one has it could be too late to swerve or turn. The mind is also slower and doesn't react as quickly. For example, if a ball rolls out into the road with a child following it, a driver would have to step on the brake and turn the wheel hard. He or she would have to make sure they didn't hit anyone coming the other way. Younger drivers have faster reflexes to do all of these things. Growing up with video games also helps. Young people practice reacting quickly on the computer for years before

they get their licenses. For example, an opponent might jump out from any angle and try
to shoot the player. He has to react quickly to save himself. Some video games even have
a car that the player drives and has to swerve out of the way of obstacles.

Ms. P: Rob, we're in the home stretch here. Great job changing all the second person "you's" into third person.

Rob: Thanks.

Ms. P: Let's look at a couple small spots in the second paragraph, and see if we can't tighten them up a bit. It will save you some revising later.

Rob: Okay.

Ms. P: First, look at your third and fifth sentences. Read them out loud for me.

Rob: Um, "Driving uses both these skills." . . . "Driving uses reflexes so the driver can quickly react to a problem."

Ms. P: What do you notice? Anything similar? *(Rather than just telling him what to do, I want him to identify it himself.)*

Rob: They both use "use"?

Ms. P: Yes, and even more than that. They both use "driving."

Rob: Oh, right.

Ms. P: Remember the rule about starting sentences the same way?

Rob: Yeah . . . don't do it in a paragraph.

Ms. P: Exactly. In addition, look at what you're saying. In the third sentence, you say that driving uses both eyesight and reflexes, right? Then in the fifth sentence you say again, "Driving uses reflexes." Does that make sense?

Rob: Oh! No. I repeated the same thing.

Ms. P: Right. I'd suggest making "reflexes" the subject and first word of that fifth sentence. That way, you have a sentence about eyesight followed by a sentence about reflexes, and you solve the problem of starting two sentences the same way in a paragraph.

Rob: So, it would be "Reflexes can quickly react"— no, um . . . "Reflexes can help you quickly react to a problem."

Ms. P: Right. Now say it again without the second person.

Rob: "Reflexes can help a person quickly react to a problem."

Ms. P: Excellent! That's it. Jot it down before you forget. *(He does.)* Now look at that sentence again about the eyesight. Notice anything with the first word?

Rob: Oh, it's a banned word.

Ms. P: Right. What's another word that would fit there?

Rob: "Poor"?

Ms. P: Exactly. Write it down. *(He does.)* Now, skim down through the paragraph. You give an

As usual, I'm minimizing the amount of work that needs to be done and trying to make Rob feel like I'm on his side. Rob has used a couple of banned words; I would never scold him for this, since I know how hard he's worked on this piece already. He also has two sentences that basically begin the same way. I will help him revise these and then let the rest of the paper go. If I find anything else when grading, I will circle it, but as always, I am trying to simply plant the seeds of habitual thinking, not perfect every single piece.

I'm making it easy for him to answer my question, while still having him identify the problem himself.

example and describe what reflexes would be needed—good job on the specifics, by the way—and then you say, "Young drivers have faster reflexes to do all of these things."

Rob: "Things."

Ms. P: Right. What exactly do you mean there? Look at the sentences before it.

Rob: Hm . . . "actions"?

Ms. P: Sure, "actions" would work there. Think of one other word.

Rob: Uh . . . "movements"?

Ms. P: Perfect. You can choose which of those you like best. Then just print out a fresh copy and you're ready to hand it in.

Rob: Okay.

Ms. P: Great work, Rob.

Rob: Thanks.

> **STRATEGY**
>
> *Have students think of at least two other words to replace a weak word.*

Sometimes I have students come up with at least two words to replace a banned word, for a couple of reasons. First, I want to demonstrate that they have an abundance of words to choose from. When students just grasp at the first word that comes to mind, it reinforces the feeling that words are a scarcity, and that if they find one that could possibly fit, they better snatch it up. There's a desperate and almost fearful quality to it. Hopefully, I can get them to relax and see that a plethora of words exists, and they can calmly choose from among them. Doing so will help to make them feel more in charge, more like an author, and less like a student anxiously trying to guess the right answer. Second, the first word that pops into their heads is not always the most effective one. It might be just as obvious or empty as the banned word itself. Pushing students one thought further can get them into richer territory.

PERSUASIVE ESSAY

Strengthening Weak Words

Students often use words that may not be officially banned, but are not as strong as they could be. Depending on time, revisions done so far, and the student's ability, I will point out such words and help him revise it. The next example is an essay against censorship in music. Part of it appears below:

> *In addition, words and writing are also some of the better ways of self expression. Songs and writings should be viewed as a way to relieve stress or anger as well as a way of putting out a message. An angry person should write a poem or song to express themselves, as opposed to physically hurting another person.*

Ms. P: Kyle, let's look at this paragraph closely. I was a bit confused the first time I read it, and I think I've pinpointed why.

Kyle: Okay.

Ms. P: The first time I read it, I wasn't sure where that very first sentence was directing me. I didn't know what exactly the paragraph was going to be about. By the end I did, but it took the whole paragraph to figure it out, and then I had to reread it. Can you guess which word in that first sentence is bringing the whole paragraph down?

Kyle: Um . . .

Ms. P: It's not exactly a banned word, but it's related to one.

Kyle: Uh . . .

Ms. P: It's not "good," not "best," but—

Kyle: Oh! "Better"?

Ms. P: Yes. It's a form of "good," isn't it? Now, it's not incorrect or ungrammatical or anything, but it's a lost chance to use a more meaningful word that could make the whole paragraph clearer. Think about your paragraph. What's a more specific word there?

Kyle: Um . . .

> *I'm not sure if he's confused or he just can't think of anything.*

Ms. P: Let me give you an example. Since the "worse" way of self-expression, according to your paragraph, involves violence, the "better" way would be nonviolent. *(I underline "better" and write "nonviolent" in the margin.)*

Kyle: Oh, right. I see.

Ms. P: That's just one example. Now, you think of one more word to add to this list, and then choose one. Do you see how changing one single word to be more specific improves the whole paragraph?

Kyle: Yes. I should think of another?

Ms. P: Yes, then choose. When you hand in your paper, I'll flip to this draft to see what you came up with. Okay?

Kyle: Okay. I'll try.

Ms. P: You'll definitely think of something. You can use the thesaurus if you want.

Kyle: Okay.

> *Although I sometimes give students time to think on the spot, I also let them think on their own. I will gladly start them with a few ideas when needed—I see it as modeling rather than "telling the answer"—but I will ask them to participate as well. In Kyle's case, this meant adding another word to my idea and having him choose the one he liked best. The process reinforces the idea that he's the author and ultimate decision maker for his piece.*

AUTOBIOGRAPHY

Revising Clichés

Because changing a cliché is not as simple as substituting one word for another, clichés are a bit harder to revise. A cliché represents a complete thought, and is often so ingrained that students do not know how to formulate the thought otherwise. With banned words, the student must dig a little deeper to find the more specific word. With some clichés, though, there is no benefit to digging deeper. New words must be strung together to formulate a new thought to replace the cliché. In the following conversation, the student has written a memoir essay about receiving her cat as a tiny kitten. After describing the anticipation, the excitement, and the wait all afternoon for her grandmother to arrive with the kitten, she ends the essay as follows:

> *She was just as I had pictured her: a small ball of fur, two pointed ears, a tiny black nose, and devilish green eyes. I put her on the couch, and she started to walk. Every step she took, she would stumble. She climbed onto my lap, and started to bite with her little sharp teeth. I knew at that minute that she would be a beast—and she still is.*
>
> *I look back on that day, and think about how long I waited. But sometimes, our best treasures take longer to arrive.*

Ms. P: Jill, I know you put a lot of effort into the brainstorming, and it worked—you have some wonderful details throughout the essay, and in the ending too.

Jill: Thanks.

Ms. P: Let's just take a look at your last paragraph, specifically the last sentence—"our best treasures take longer to arrive." That phrase is a cliché. Do you remember what that means?

Jill: No . . . is it like a banned word?

Ms. P: Yes, yes, exactly like it. Flip back in your notebook to the mini-lesson on clichés, and skim through the list. *(She does.)* Remember?

Jill: Oh, it's like a phrase you say all the time.

Ms. P: Right, it's those phrases we all use when talking. The problem is, in writing they don't really have much power. Your job as a writer is to always use your own words, not phrases everyone uses. Does that make sense?

Jill: Sure. Okay, I'll change it.

When Jill next turns in the paper, the last paragraph reads:

> *I look back at that day, and think about how long I waited. But I knew Blackie was worth the wait.*

This illustrates my earlier point about revising clichés—often a student does not know where to turn and simply replaces one cliché with another. Since this paragraph was the conclusion of her essay, I decide to direct her back to her theme, which she alluded to earlier in the essay but did not fully explore.

> *I'm using a chiding rather than a scolding tone.*

Ms. P: Jill, you revised the cliché but, I'm afraid, with another cliché. Don't you hear people all the time say, "It was worth the wait"?

Jill: *(She chuckles.)* Oh, yeah, I guess so.

Ms. P: It has some nice alliteration in it, doesn't it, with the two "w's" in "worth" and "wait." That's why people like to say it. But it's still a cliché.

> *I really do make observations like this to students. I'll use anything I can to foster awareness of their own writing and of literary terms.*

Jill: What else can I write? I couldn't think of anything.

Ms. P: Well, why don't you look again at your theme?

Jill: This *is* part of my theme—I learned to wait. That's what I learned from the experience.

Ms. P: That's good, and an important moment. Let's try this: Put that idea to the side for a moment, and go back to you sitting on the couch with Blackie. You're looking back now from the present to when she was a kitten. What if, for the conclusion, you brought us into the present and had her sitting on your lap as a cat?

Jill: Huh . . . yeah, that could work.

Ms. P: I think so. Especially since you have all that wonderful description in the preceding paragraph of her as a kitten. Stay in the moment with Blackie. Use details. Don't pull back. Using clichés is a way of backing away from the real action. Don't do that. Force yourself to stay in the moment with Blackie, even if that moment jumps ahead a few years.

Jill: I could compare her now to then.

Ms. P: Sure. And don't write out the "learning to wait" idea. Let the details speak for themselves. Let the details point to a theme. See what happens.

Jill: Okay. I'll try.

Ms. P: Good!

STRATEGY

Push students to stay in the moment by using details in lieu of clichés.

Explaining to students, or even demonstrating to them, that writing is an exploration is no easy task. If a writer stays close to the moment and details, the writing will make *itself* glimmer with dimension. Too often, students use clichés to add that extra layer of thought and "truth," but they must learn instead to trust the process of writing. Jill's revision of her final paragraph appears below:

> As I sit on the same couch now with Blackie, I realize how important she is to me. She no longer walks like a kitten but lays stretched out, her black fur long and still soft. She looks at me with those same devilish green eyes and swats at keys I hold in front of her. She knows me now and I know her. She is mine.

Ms. P: Jill, this is wonderful, and so much better than "our best treasures take longer to arrive"! Do you see what I mean now by staying close to the moment? You leave the reader with an image of Blackie.

Jill: Yes. And it wasn't that hard to think of details about her, since I hold her every day.

Ms. P: That's the thing—it seems like it would be more work to push yourself to look more closely at a moment or person or, in your case, a pet, but when you settle down and get into it, it's not so hard.

Jill: Yeah.

Ms. P: Let's look at two verbs that are a bit average. They're not incorrect or anything, but if they were stronger the reader would get a more definite picture of Blackie. I'm thinking of "walks" and "hold." *(I underline the two verbs.)*

Jill: Oh, yeah, I forgot about "walk"—we have that list. *(She is referring to the mini-lesson "Words Instead of 'Walk.'")*

Ms. P: Right. That's a chance to really give us a clear image of Blackie. You use "stumble" in the previous paragraph, so think of something like that, but a different word. You can consult the list in your notebook. Same idea with "hold"—another word could be more specific.

Jill: How about "dangle"?

Ms. P: Perfect.

Jill: And for "walks," um . . .

Ms. P: You don't have to answer now. Think about it, check the list, and I'll see your decision when you hand in the essay. Okay? Good work, Jill.

Jill: Okay. Thanks.

Jill turns in the paper with "wobbles" as the delightful revision for "walks." With just a little more effort, Jill replaced the cliché with an ending that strengthened the entire essay. This happens often with a cliché: Sometimes the sentences around it, or even the entire paragraph, need to be revised. Sometimes a cliché can simply be cut or replaced with a more meaningful phrase, but at times its presence indicates the need for a more widespread overhaul.

BOOK REVIEW

Condensing Weak Verbs

Verbs are the heart of our language. They pulse with movement and push the rest of the piece through its channels, which I stress throughout the year. When a sentence contains a strong verb, the rest of the words take their places around it. If students concentrate on nothing but using strong verbs for most sentences, their writing will improve. One trick I tell them is to check for verbs that require a second word, usually either an adverb or preposition, and try to think of a single verb that expresses the same idea. For example, instead of saying "work hard," one could write "struggle." Some verb phrases even involve a third word. Not all of these verb combinations can be avoided or revised, but some can. By habitually scrutinizing verb choices writers can strengthen their skills at formulating verbs at the thought-moment.

Though students rarely detect these two-part verb phrases on their own, I try to point them out when appropriate. With more advanced students, I can devote more time to this practice since they require less instruction in other areas. Here is the beginning of a student's book review of *The Outsiders*:

> *Imagine taking part in the death of somebody. That is exactly what happened to a boy named Johnny who was a Greaser in S. E. Hinton's* The Outsiders.

Samantha's paper was well-organized and had the requisite quotation from the book as well as adequate examples. I met with her earlier about her ideas, so at this point, I am ready to look closely at specific parts of the essay.

Ms. P: Samantha, let's look at the introduction. I like how you started with the word "imagine" in order to involve the reader. You don't start by giving us the background or any other fluff; you just seize one of the most important points in the story. Good idea.

Samantha: Thanks.

Ms. P: Let's examine the language in that first sentence, because I think it could be even more gripping and intriguing. What's your verb?

Samantha: Um . . . "taking"?

Ms. P: Yes, but you don't mean "taking" as in "I'm taking another piece of pizza," right? What's the whole verb phrase?

Samantha: "taking part"?

Ms. P: Right, and you could even add the word "in" to that, depending on how you view the grammar of the sentence. Now, the more words it takes to say something, the weaker it will be. A general rule in writing is that it is better to use fewer, stronger words than to use many weak, small words. Does that make sense?

Samantha: Yes. *(I don't know if I believe her.)*

Ms. P: For example, what would be a better way to say this: "I spoke so softly that my voice didn't come out and I used only air."

Samantha: "Whispered"?

Ms. P: Right, "I whispered." See how one strong word replaces all those other words? How about this one: "I walked around the bike." What one word could mean "walked around"?

> I purposely gave her an easy example followed by a more challenging one.

Samantha: Um . . .

Ms. P: Think of a shape.

Samantha: "Circled"?

Ms. P: Right! Exactly. See how "I circled the bike" has more meaning in fewer words?

> I'm leading her but I want her to make the final connection.

Samantha :   Yes.

Ms. P: That's what you want to do whenever you can. Now let's look again at "taking part in."

Samantha: How about "participating in"?

Ms. P: That's definitely better. Tell me exactly what you mean about Johnny.

Samantha: Well, I was thinking of the part where the Socs were drowning Ponyboy and Johnny shoots the guy who is doing it. He didn't mean to kill anybody. He just did it without thinking, trying to save Ponyboy.

Ms. P:	Okay. So even though he didn't plan it, he was totally responsible for the soc's death, right? So maybe another word that is stronger than "participating in" would be appropriate for that first sentence. Can you think of any?
Samantha:	I thought of "killing" before, but I don't want that, because it sounds like he meant to do it.
Ms. P:	I agree. Besides, most readers wouldn't be able to imagine the act of killing someone.
Samantha:	Yeah, um . . . how about "causing the death of someone while trying to save your friend"?
Ms. P:	Good—you can certainly expand the sentence if you want. Look what you did to the verb, though—you went from "taking part in" to "causing." See how it says more with less?
Samantha:	Uh-huh. *(She writes the phrase in the margin.)*
Ms. P:	Good. I would say "in order to save your friend" so that it seems like there was no other choice.
Samantha:	And maybe it should be a *best* friend.
Ms. P:	Yes. Now, can you get rid of, I mean, eradicate—since we're trying to use fewer words—can you eradicate "of" in that sentence?
Samantha:	Um . . . "Imagine causing someone's death"?
Ms. P:	Excellent. Now read the whole sentence to me.
Samantha:	"Imagine causing someone's death in order to save your best friend."
Ms. P:	Much stronger. Good work.
Samantha:	Thanks.
Ms. P:	I want you to find one more verb in this paper to strengthen in the same way, and from now on, I want you to add "Strengthen two verbs" to your Editing/Revising Checksheet for all future assignments. Okay?
Samantha:	Okay.

I can't go through a whole paper in that way, but I try to pinpoint sentences here and there that can serve as examples students will hopefully remember. For every sentence I revise with a student, there may be three more I let be, for the sake of time.

CHARACTER SKETCH

Changing Linking Verbs to Actions

The following student, Nick, wrote a character sketch about his grandmother after completing an extensive prewriting exercise. He included many details about his grandmother, and tried to give a meaningful portrayal of her doing what she loves, cooking. However, due to lackluster language, the essay felt general and unexceptional. Two of the middle paragraphs appear below:

She is a short old lady with curly hair and glasses. Her eyes are soft brown and when she is happy she winks at me. Sometimes she doesn't have to say a word and I can tell that she is in a terrific mood. There is one problem with her. She smokes too much and nobody can convince her to quit.

Dinner is cooking in the kitchen. She loves to cook and she likes to make other people happy. It seems like all she does is cook. I take a smell of the air and mmmm, this smells delicious. She is making her famous chicken cutlets. It will be a fabulous meal.

Ms. P: Nick, as I told you during the prewriting, you have many touching details in here about your grandmother. I love how you begin it with yourself coming home from school and "Grammie" is making jokes as you walk through the door.

Nick: Yeah, she always does that.

Ms. P: You're obviously very close to her.

Nick: Yes.

Ms. P: She lives with your family then?

Nick: Yeah, she moved in about four years ago when my pappy died. It's been great having her.

Ms. P: Well, Nick, I think that's wonderful. You're lucky to be so close to her, both physically and emotionally. A lot of kids don't have that.

Nick: I know.

Ms. P: Let's take a look at the essay—you have a strong intro and conclusion. The whole scene is organized well, and I feel like the details really give me a sense of your grandmother. In some places, though, your language is a little flat. It's not jumping out at me. And I think Grammie deserves the most vivid writing we can muster, don't you?

Nick: Definitely.

> *I'm trying to reinforce his emotional investment in the piece.*

Ms. P: Okay, look at your second paragraph. You have some wonderful details—the curly hair, the glasses, the soft brown eyes. However, it reads like a list. Part of the reason is your verbs. What are your verbs in those first two sentences?

Nick: Um . . . "is" in the first and . . . "winks"?

Ms. P: *(I circle "is.")* You're right, but you skipped a couple verbs in that second sentence. Look again.

Nick: Oh, um, "is"—

Ms. P: And one more; keep backing up to the beginning of the sentence. *(Nick looks.)*

Nick: I can't find it.

Ms. P: If I said, "One eye *is* brown," I would say, "*Two eyes* . . ." *(I want him to find it.)*

Nick: Oh! "Are."

Ms. P: Good. "Are" sometimes slips by because we're always looking for "is," right? Okay, so we have "is," "are," and "is," and then "winks." The first three are linking verbs, meaning that they have no action. That's what makes it feel like a list. But the reader wants action. It's tricky, though, when you're trying to get in as many details as possible. You don't want to say something like "She grows hair," right?

Nick: No.

Ms. P: Right. That sounds silly and forced. Let's go back to your scene. You come in from school and Grammie's cooking dinner or doing some other task in the kitchen. Can you have her doing something, and then bring in the hair and glasses? For example, maybe she's chopping something fast or scrubbing something hard, and her curls bob gently. See? That makes "bob" your verb, and it's much more vivid.

Nick: Yes. Okay. *(He writes, "Curls bob—cutting? washing?" in the margin.)*

Ms. P: You could even just say, "Her hair curls around her glasses." Then the verb is curls—it's an action, and more interesting. See?

I'm both modeling my thought process and giving him several choices so that he feels he has many options.

Nick: Yeah. *(He writes, "Curls as verb.")*

Ms. P: Now, what about the glasses? Can you think of something in the kitchen that would happen to them? Does she move them or put them down somewhere?

Nick: No, but every time she checks a pot of spaghetti on the stove, they steam up. It's funny. I always laugh at her.

Ms. P: That's perfect, Nick! Jot that down. Now, "winks" is great, but instead of saying she is happy, how can you show she is happy?

Nick: She smiles?

Ms. P: Exactly. Maybe after her glasses clear, she smiles and winks without saying a word. Then, you can cut "she is in a terrific mood" because we will already know that. See what I'm doing? Instead of *telling* us all these characteristics of your grandmother, you can *show* us by staying in the scene.

Nick: Yeah. Okay. What about the cigarettes?

Ms. P: Well, you tell me. How can you *show* she is a smoker?

Nick: She usually has a pack of cigarettes on a shelf next to the microwave.

Ms. P: Perfect. Now, in that next paragraph, you can pretty much jump straight to the smelling— since you already *showed* us in the first two sentences, we don't need them. *(I cross them out.)* But look at your description of the smells—you use words like "delicious," "fabulous," and . . . "mmmm"? *(Nick laughs.)*

Nick: I didn't know what else to put.

Ms. P: Well, your job as the writer is to figure it out. What *are* the smells? Can you identify them?

Nick: The chicken?

Ms. P: Anything else? Butter? Garlic? Cheese?

Nick: Definitely garlic. Maybe . . . onions?

Ms. P: Maybe that's what she could be chopping in the paragraph before it. Maybe garlic and onion are frying in butter—I can almost taste it! Then you wouldn't have to use words like "delicious" and "fabulous"—I would already be thinking it. Words like "delicious" and "fabulous" are hard to imagine. They're like banned words: everyone uses them for everything, so they're not very specific.

Nick: What about "is" in the last sentence? Do I have to change that?

Ms. P: Actually, no. That "is" is a helping verb for "making." The main verb is "make" and adding "is" shows that it's in progress. It's not a linking verb in that sentence. But good question.

Nick: Okay.

Ms. P: I'm going to circle a couple other spots here that have either linking verbs or general words that need more description, and you just see what you can do with them. Just stay in the moment, and keep picturing Grammie in action. Think you can do it?

Nick: Yes, okay.

Ms. P: Great. Excellent work, Nick.

ANALYSIS OF A POEM

Eradicating Linking Verbs by Combining Sentences

Similar to Nick's case, Chris's essay on John Updike's "Sonic Boom" contains many linking verbs. Instead of converting them to active verbs, however, the best solution here involves cutting and combining sentences. Here is Chris's first paragraph:

> *Have you ever heard a plane break the speed of sound? Like a lot of people, I have never heard a sonic boom. I can only imagine what it sounds like. The title of this poem is "Sonic Boom." The author is John Updike. This poem is about a man calming a child who is afraid when he hears a sonic boom, he explains to the child that their world is very tame. That's not the only thing this poem is about though, there is a hidden meaning that does not really surface till the end of the poem.*

He went on to describe the onomatopoeia throughout the poem, the rhyme scheme, the meter, and the poem's theme. He had an adequate understanding of the poem, but his weak language overshadowed his knowledge.

Ms. P: Chris, I'm glad you liked this poem so much. And you give an insightful analysis of it, especially with all the examples of onomatopoeia in the second paragraph.

Chris: I just think it's really cool.

Ms. P: The idea or the poem?

Chris: Both!

Ms. P: John Updike is clever, isn't he? He's one of the most prolific writers living today—meaning, he's really written a lot—dozens of novels, hundreds of poems, essays, and stories. It's amazing.

Chris: Wow. That's a lot of writing.

Ms. P: It is, but I'm sure he has gotten a lot of help over the years from teachers and friends. And, needless to say, he works very hard. Now, let's take a look at your first paragraph. You start with a question, and then give some facts about the poem. The facts themselves are helpful, so the reader has all the necessary information heading into the essay. But look at your verbs. *(I circle all the instances of "is.")*

> *I'm trying to portray Updike as human.*

Chris: Uh-oh. Oh boy.

Ms. P: Right. The effect is very choppy. Any ideas?

Chris: Um . . . I should make it an action, so how about "John Updike titled his poem 'Sonic Boom.'"

Ms. P: You're on the right track, Chris, but take it even further. What's the *main* action of the poem, and your paragraph? Is it that Updike merely gave the poem a title?

Chris: No . . . in the poem, it's that the man calms the son, like I say in the next sentence.

Ms. P: Right. So make that action the main verb, and put the author and title in with it. Combine all three sentences together.

Chris: All three? So it would be "John Updike wrote 'Sonic Boom,' and it is a poem about a man calming a child—"

Ms. P: You're getting closer. Take out "is." Don't say "and it is a poem." Remember, the main action is not that Updike *wrote* it, but that *in* it a man *calms* a child, like you just said. Start with "in," and use "calms" as your main verb.

Chris: Um . . . "In 'Sonic Boom,' written by John Updike, a man calms a child."

Ms. P: Much better. You could even take out the "written" if you want, but I'll let you decide on that.

Chris: Oh, just say "by John Updike." That's even shorter.

Ms. P: Yes. Shorter, but we preserved all the information that you originally had in three sentences. Do you see the effect? We condensed it all down and now, instead of three choppy, weak sentences, we have one strong one with the most meaning. You see, readers don't like reading a lot of weak words with little meaning—it's like doing a lot of work and not getting much in return. When you see a lot of "is" sentences in your paper, a red flag should go up in your mind. The fewer words, the better. I want you to comb through the rest of the paper and circle all the "is" verbs—the linking verbs, I mean— and ask yourself what you can do about them. Limit yourself to one linking verb per paragraph. *(I write "Circle all linking verbs" at the top of the draft.)*

Chris: Got it.

Ms. P: That includes "am," "was," "are," and "were." And "be," "being," and "been." Just look up at the "Linking Verb" poster if you forget. And for the next several assignments, I want you to write, "Check for linking verbs," on your E/R Check Sheets. Okay?

Chris: Okay.

Ms. P: Now, let's look at that last sentence. You're trying to say that there is a twist at the end, but your language is so vague that it doesn't give any clue to grasp on to. You even have a banned word in there.

Chris: I do? Oh, "thing." I didn't know what else to put there.

Ms. P: Tell me what the "hidden meaning" is you're thinking of.

Chris: Well, at the end, he says something like, if the world does end with a pop, meaning a nuclear explosion, he won't look up to see it drop.

Ms. P: Excellent paraphrasing! What does it mean?

Chris: That the world is tame, but if it were going to end, there's nothing he can do about it anyway. He'll just stay focused on his life and if it ends, it ends.

Ms. P: Excellent! So he's determined to live without fear, is that it? . . . . *I'm trying to give him words to use.*

Chris: Yes.

Ms. P: This idea, combined with the sentence before it, would constitute your thesis, don't you think? *(I bracket the two sentences on his paper.)*

Chris: Well, yes . . . I was thinking the first sentence you mentioned is the thesis, but I can see how this idea about the end of the poem is part of it too.

Ms. P: Right. With a thesis, Chris, you have go a little bit further than stating the obvious. You have to take a risk. I think your idea about the ending might just do it. Now, how can you state what you think about the ending without giving it all away?

Chris: Let's see . . . something like, "At the end of the poem, the man tells what he really thinks about the world"?

Ms. P: Something like that, yes. Keep working on it—start the sentence with what you just said: "At the end of the poem, the man," then keep tinkering with the rest.

Chris: Okay. *(He writes the beginning in the margin.)*

Ms. P: You have a wonderful understanding of the poem, Chris. Keep working on the draft and I'll check back after you turn it in, alright?

Chris: Okay. Thanks.

After Chris turns in the draft, I'll help him fix the many run-ons throughout the essay. Right now, he's got a big enough job revising the linking verbs.

INTRODUCTORY LETTER

Converting Passive Voice to Active

In my experience, middle school students don't usually overuse the passive voice. I've had to help students revise a paragraph with too much passive voice, but not often. Here is one such example. It occurred during the first assignment of the year, which was to write an introductory letter. The student is describing herself, and the emphasis on "I" throughout the letter naturally leads her to slip into the passive. Following is one of the middle paragraphs:

I have won a few awards in the past few years. In sixth grade, I was given an award for community service. My family and me were invited to a special dinner for all the honorees, and I was given a plaque. In seventh grade, I was given a certificate for perfect attendance. That same year, my softball team also were runners-up in our tournament and we were presented with a second-place trophy.

Ms. P: Kim, the entire letter is well-organized; each paragraph has one topic and examples to go with it. Great job so far.

Kim: Thanks.

Ms. P: The main issue going on in the letter is something we call "passive voice." Have you ever heard of that?

Kim: No.

Ms. P: Let me give you an example—I'll use softball since you play it. "Kim threw the softball." *(I write it at the top of her page.)* Who's the thrower?

Kim: Me.

Ms. P: Right. What is being thrown?

Kim: The ball.

Ms. P: Right. The sentence is in the active voice, meaning the subject, which is usually the first word of the sentence or somewhere near there, is doing the action. "Kim" is the subject; "Kim" is doing the action. Get it so far?

Kim: Yes.

Ms. P: Okay. Now, let's keep the same idea, that Kim throws the ball, but switch around the words. "The ball was thrown by Kim." *(I write it below the first.)* Same idea, right?

Kim: Yes.

Ms. P: But what is the subject this time? Look at the beginning of the sentence.

Kim: Um, the ball?

Ms. P: Exactly. That's the passive voice. We flipped it around so that the thrower—Kim—is at the end of the sentence instead of the beginning. Now, look at the two verbs: "threw" and "was thrown." What's the difference between them?

Kim: The "was"?

Ms. P: Excellent. Passive voice always has an extra word like "was," "were," "is," "am," or "are." Do you understand? *(I write the verbs on her paper.)*

Kim: Yes, I think so.

Ms. P: Good. Now here's the rule: active voice is better than passive. It's more exciting for the reader. *(I star our first example on her paper.)*

Kim: Okay.

> *I'm hoping this rudimentary explanation won't intimidate her. As the year progresses, I can fine-tune her understanding.*

Ms. P: Let's look at one of your paragraphs in the middle of the letter. Almost all of it is in passive voice. Let's see if we can change some of them. Your first sentence is fine: "I have won a few awards." "I" is the subject and "I" did the winning. But look at the next sentence: "I was given an award." It's in the passive voice, because you didn't give the award to someone else, right?

Kim: No, they gave it to me.

Ms. P: Right. So to switch around the sentence, we have to know who gave it to you.

Kim: My Girl Scout troop.

Ms. P: Oh! Isn't that interesting! So already, we have some new, more interesting information than we did before. Okay, see if you can reword that sentence starting with "In sixth grade, my Girl Scout troop."

Kim: "In sixth grade, my Girl Scout troop . . . gave me an award for community service"?

Ms. P: Excellent! Now look at the next sentence. What's the verb?

Kim: "Invited"?

Ms. P: Well, "were invited." It's passive. Who did the inviting?

Kim: The Girl Scouts.

Ms. P: Okay, so rewrite the sentence using "the Girl Scouts" in the beginning of the sentence instead of "my family and me."

Kim: "The Girl Scouts invited my family and me to a special dinner"?

Ms. P: Perfect! Now, let's look at the next sentence.

Kim: "I was given a certificate" would be "The school gave me a certificate."

Ms. P: Excellent, Kim! You've got it! Jot that down. Now, look at the very end of the paragraph: "we were presented with a second place trophy." Instead of flipping the doer and the receiver, let's try to change the verb entirely. What is the verb in that phrase?

Kim: Um . . . "presented"?

Ms. P: That's half of it, yes. Remember, it's in the passive.

Kim: Oh—"were presented"?

Ms. P: Right. Now, what other verb can you put in that sentence, without using "were"? *(I cross out "were presented with" in the paragraph.)* Look at the words that are left. What would fit there?

Kim: Let's see . . . "we" . . . um . . . "we got a second place trophy"?

Ms. P: Good! That's the idea. Now, think of another one.

Kim: Another? Um . . . "we won a second place trophy"?

> *I'm purposely ignoring the "plaque" half of the "dinner" sentence because the passive voice seems appropriate there. If she asks, I'll explain to her why I think so, but for right now I want to keep her focused on how to convert passive to active; I don't want to confuse her with how to determine when the passive voice is effective and when it is not. Later in the year we can have that discussion.*

Ms. P: You got it! "Won" is stronger than "got." Do you see what we did? We changed the subject from the receiver to the doer. Instead of someone presenting you with something, you won something. It's more interesting that way. Do you understand?

Kim: I think so.

Ms. P: In the next few assignments, I want you to think about passive voice as you are writing, and to check for it after you're done writing, okay? I'll help you; before long it will seem easy.

Kim: Okay.

Ms. P: Great work, Kim.

Kim: Thanks.

The ideas about language that we are discussing here will have to be reinforced again and again through subsequent conferences, the Editing/Revising Check Sheets, and the grading rubric. Most people cannot assimilate new information the first time they hear it, much less immediately begin to use it in their work. The process takes the entire year, and many concepts take much longer than that. The results of my efforts often surface two or three teachers later.

What to Call It: Finding Titles

Most students have no idea what they will end up naming their essays, even at the later stages. A few will need a working title in order to start the piece (I tell them to write whatever they can think of and revise it later) but in general, titles are not a major concern. That's why I tend to save in-depth work on titles for the very end.

From the beginning of the year, I require the students to title their essays, but we don't do a mini-lesson on titles until the second quarter. In the mini-lesson, I ask what qualities characterize an interesting title. Usually students can come up with a few ideas, as well as some titles of books and movies that they like.

EFFECTIVE TITLES

- Get the reader's attention
- Tell something about the topic
- May give information not included in the piece
- Pique curiosity
- Allude to the theme

I have students examine the images and themes in their writing and see if they can make some connections. As with all other aspects of writing, I can best coach the students one-on-one with a particular piece of writing in front of us.

AUTOBIOGRAPHY

Using Theme and Imagery

After the mini-lesson on titles, I have students retrieve the permanent folders where their finished work is kept. I then spend a class helping them revise their titles. Students usually enjoy a break from the routine of the workshop, and since the papers in their permanent folders have already received final grades, the pressure is off. (This exercise can count as extra credit in classes that need either points or motivation.)

When Lauren revisits her memoir essay about seeing fireworks with her dad, she realizes its title, "Fireworks," isn't very effective.

Ms. P: Any ideas yet, Lauren? *(I see she has her notebook open to the mini-lesson on titles.)*

Lauren: Not really. Just things like "Watching the Fireworks" or "My Dad, Brother and I."

Ms. P: Okay, let's take another look at the piece. It is so well-crafted and rich with details and meaning. You really did a nice job on it.

Lauren: Thanks.

Ms. P: In all of your title ideas so far, you do give important bits of information that relate to the story, and that's good. But they don't seem catchy enough, right?

Lauren: No, nothing that would make someone want to read it again.

Ms. P: Tell me the theme again, in your own words.

Lauren: I was upset with my dad because I thought he never lets me do anything, but then I realized he had this nice surprise for me and my brother.

Ms. P: Okay. So some important words could be "Dad" and "surprise." I write them at the top of her paper. What are some of the important images in the story? Skim through.

Lauren: Um . . . well, the fireworks . . . the water, the canoe . . . the other partyers . . . the light on my dad's face . . . him smiling. *(I write the nouns from each of her phrases in a list on her paper.)*

Ms. P: Okay, Lauren. Try this: just look at this list of your own words. Play around with them, and try to put two or three of them together and see what you come up with.

Lauren: How do you mean?

Ms. P: Well, something like, "Canoe Surprise" or "Fireworks on the Water"—not either of those, though; they're not good enough. But make a list that combines these words. Don't worry if any of the phrases are the perfect title or not; just make the list. You can fill in other words if you need to, and you can use -ing or -s or any other forms of the words. *(I write "-ing" and "'s" on her paper.)* And if any new phrase pops into your mind, write that too.

Lauren: I'll try.

Ms. P: Good. I'll check back.

> This exercise gives Lauren some concrete material to work with, while also leaving the possibility for free association. It makes the task seem less nebulous and takes the pressure off; this relaxes the mind while simultaneously occupying it, leaving space for new ideas to "pop in."

When I do, her list reads:

Dad Smiling
Smiling Water
~~*Smiling Light*~~
Smiles in Light
Water Surprise
Fireworks Over the Canoe
Fireworks Surprise
Light Surprise
Smiling Fireworks
Faces of Light

Ms. P: How'd you do?

Lauren: I got some, but I don't know if they're any good.

Ms. P: You have some interesting ones here. Which ones do you like?

Lauren: I like "Smiles in Light" and "Fireworks Surprise" best, and maybe "Dad Smiling."

> *I resist telling her which ones I like.*

Ms. P: You did seem to focus on the word "smiling." Why do you like those best?

Lauren: Well, my dad and me smiling is that moment at the end—

Ms. P: Good! So those titles point to the theme, right?

Lauren: Yes. And I like the idea of light, because the fireworks are light.

Ms. P: I love the idea of light, Lauren, because the image is light in darkness—you're surrounded by darkness and light flashes through. It's symbolic of your theme. The darkness is your being angry at your dad, and the light is your realizing he just cares.

Lauren: Wow, I didn't even think of that.

Ms. P: So which do you think you want to go with?

Lauren: Maybe "Smiles in Light" since it has two meanings, like you said in the mini-lesson.

Ms. P: What are they?

Lauren: Well, one of the fireworks was a smiley face, and then at the end me and my dad smiled in the light. Do those count?

Ms. P: Sure, and I think that title piques the reader's curiosity too. And, as a bonus, it has some nice assonance with the long "i" sound—smiiiiles and liiiight. I like it. Good job!

> *As always, I seize the chance to reinforce her understanding of a literary technique and give her credit for using it.*

Lauren: Thanks. *(She crosses out the old title and writes the new one above it.)*

I am satisfied that Lauren has fulfilled the criteria for an effective title. What she learned through this exercise she can practice all year.

Using the Thesis

Rob had originally titled his persuasive piece about retesting older drivers "Young or Old?" (see page 51 for the full version). After he revises and corrects the organization, language, and grammar, I ask him about the title.

Ms. P: Okay, Rob, this piece has really shaped up into a clear, convincing argument.

Rob: Thanks.

Ms. P: The only part that doesn't do the work it should is the title.

Rob: I know. I thought of it first when I started writing and never changed it.

Ms. P: Well, I can tell that you tried to rouse the reader's curiosity by making it a question, but it's still a bit vague. And it doesn't point to the main idea of your essay, which is that older drivers should be retested.

Rob: So I should change it?

Ms. P: I think so. Do you remember the characteristics of an effective title?

Rob: Yeah . . . *(He flips through his notebook.)*

Ms. P: You want something specifically about older drivers being too slow or dangerous. You don't have to spell it out, but a title should at least point to your main idea. Try to think of at least three titles so you have something to choose from.

Rob: Should I show my position in the title? What I feel about it?

Ms. P: Like I said, Rob, you don't have to spell out your thesis, but there should be some hint of it.

Rob: Okay.

When I return to Rob's desk, he has come up with the following ideas:

> *Slow, Dangerous Drivers*
> *Go Back to the Driving Board*
> *Life in the Slow Lane*
> *Retest, Please*

Ms. P: Good work, Rob! I see you tried a straightforward one at first and then branched out. Which one do you like?

Rob: I think, "Life in the Slow Lane."

Ms. P: Good. Why?

Rob: Well, the second one is a little harsh, even though I like it. And the last one isn't catchy enough.

Ms. P: Rob, your instincts are excellent! I agree with your choice.

Rob: So it's not a cliché? I'm allowed to use it?

Ms. P: Well, "Life in the fast lane" is a cliché, but you've changed it to give it a new meaning—you've used the power of the cliché to your advantage, which is clever and effective, Rob. Also, because of that, it sounds a bit sarcastic, right?

Rob: Yeah.

Ms. P: That's the tone, and this tone reflects your position on the subject. It's great, Rob. It gives us a taste of the topic and your position, and gets our attention because it's funny. I think it's perfect.

Rob: Good. It made me think of something for the ending.

Ms. P: It did? What?

Rob: As a last sentence, I could put something like, "It's time to get older drivers up to speed."

Ms. P: That's excellent, Rob! I think it fits perfectly, and it creates a frame for the entire piece. And the tone is just right for a persuasive essay.

Rob: I thought of "get up to speed" for a title, but then I thought it could be a clincher.

Ms. P: Again, Rob, your instincts are right on. Great work. Reprint a fresh copy of the whole essay for your permanent folder.

Rob: Okay.

I don't push students on every title of every piece. Usually, their titles are of the same caliber as Rob's "Slow, Dangerous Drivers." At this stage, if students gain an awareness of a title's purpose and what goes into creating one, all I ask is that they make a few attempts and I am satisfied.

CHAPTER 11

Talking to Students About Poetry

Much of what is true for writing essays is also true for writing poetry. Compelling poems, like compelling essays, require sensory detail, staying in the moment, strong language, a deeper meaning, and effective beginnings and endings. The first major difference between poetry and prose is the white space. The form of a poem, defined by the white space around it, makes a poem a poem. We must somehow communicate to students that aside from the actual words in a poem, additional meaning resides in the white space, and the poet knows this.

The second major difference is the emphasis on sound. In prose, we do focus on the flow of language, but meaning gets more attention than sound. In poetry, sound creates meaning and also helps establish the poem's form. Of course, no writer—a poet, student or otherwise—can sloppily patch nice-sounding words together without any attention to meaning. Poems can be difficult, but they must somehow make sense. Poetry can be choppy, broken, or disjointed in ways prose usually can't. In poetry, sound can be a structure rather than chronology or reasoning, although these can certainly be used in poems as well. A deeper meaning often resides in sound that could not have been communicated otherwise. I once heard the poet Kay Ryan explain that once a word is used in a poem, its relatives—the words that rhyme with it— call to each other.

> The two main differences between poetry and prose are the *white space* and *sound.*

Before attempting to write poems, students should read and think about a number of poems by respected poets. Even with the constraints of time and curriculum, the daily study of poetry is feasible. It can be brief—one poem a day. If that is impossible, give students a packet of various poems before they begin a poetry writing assignment so they will at least have some exposure to the possibilities of form, sound, organization, and style.

To effectively guide our students, we must be familiar and comfortable with poetry, both classic and contemporary. I am always surprised at how many English teachers I meet who are completely intimidated by poetry or who can go no further into the canon than the most anthologized of Shakespearean sonnets or Coleridge's "Rime of the Ancient Mariner."

> **STRATEGY**
>
> *Reading a poem a day will familiarize students with poetry and prepare them to write.*

Students immediately sense a teacher's attitudes about poetry. If we present poetry as a normal and vital part of our daily lives and the life of our culture, our students will start to believe it too. We don't have to be experts—I frequently tell students that I never understand a poem upon first reading it, that a section or word in a certain poem still makes me struggle, that my understanding of any poem always deepens the more I read it. Nevertheless, we as teachers do have to be lovers of poetry and what it can do. The students must see this if we expect them to risk writing a poem. More than essay writing, poetry writing involves a vulnerability that we must support and protect.

When teaching poetry writing, I try to root students in sensory detail and sound. I do this by having them freewrite about a topic and then select images, details, words, and phrases to transfer to a prewriting sheet. There, they can expand their freewriting nuggets into similes or longer phrases with alliteration, toy with onomatopoeia and personification, or bring in some of those rhyming relatives. I push them to use the details they've come up with to think of even more details. I then ask them to find an interesting place to start the poem. (I do not ask them for an interesting place to end. Even more than essay writing, poetry writing is a journey that must be undertaken in order to discover the ending.) The student then approaches the blank page with this paper. I do realize that most poets don't fill out prewriting sheets before sitting to write a poem, but many of them do make notes when ideas or phrases enter their minds. I see the prewriting sheet as a jumble of notes the students can select from as they write.

When I'm helping a student with a poem, first I look at the imagery and sounds so that the poem has a strong footing. Then I look at the ending to see where we've traveled. Often, revising or adding to the imagery and sounds will uncover a stronger ending than what was there originally. Otherwise, I will try to help the student figure out what the poem is trying to say. It is more difficult to weave a theme into a poem than an essay, but even so, a poem cannot simply be a list. Even if it only obliquely glances toward a deeper meaning ("Tell all the truth but tell it with a slant"), a poem must have something that goes beyond description. Asking the student questions like "What does the speaker of this poem want?" or "What does she love?" or "What does he fear?" might help get at this something extra.

After the student and I examine the poem's language and theme, I help trim the unneeded words and tidy the line breaks. A sophisticated understanding of line breaks evolves with years of reading poems, so I don't expect students to intuitively sense where to end a line. Instead, I just give them a few basic guidelines: first, each line should contain something interesting, meaningful, or important, and second, the student should break the line with the natural phrase unless deliberately going for some specific effect. We look at poems that intentionally break a line somewhere odd and we discuss why the poet did that. Some students will try it, but most write lines by length, trying to keep the poem visually uniform. This is fine, but usually I have to help them clean up the prepositions or articles dangling in space.

> ### BASIC LINE BREAK GUIDELINES:
>
> 1. Each line should contain something interesting, meaningful, or important.
>
> 2. Unless purposely choosing not to, break the lines along natural phrases.

I keep rhyming dictionaries in the room, but I don't require that students' poems rhyme (or have a specific meter) until an assignment at the end of the year. For most of the year, I focus only on detail and internal sounds, and on deepening the meaning. Because rhyme can unlock the imagination like no other technique, I sometimes will ask a student to try to find a rhyming word for one of the words in the poem (no matter where in the poem the rhyme ends up appearing). More often, I will steer a student away from predictable, shallow rhymes that can suffocate the poem.

As with all other assignments, my goal is not perfection but progress. Students may never write poetry again after my class, but I want them to have the experience nonetheless, regardless of the outcome. I usually assign four or five poems a year, one a quarter, although students can write more if they choose to during the "free choice" assignments at the end of each quarter.

FREE VERSE

Sharpening Details; Using a Simile for an Ending; Strengthening Line Breaks

Students often write about the beach, perhaps because it evokes strong sensory detail and a sense of meaningfulness. For the following poem, Camille worked diligently on her prewriting. Her draft contains many details as well as alliteration and personification:

A Day at the Beach

The smell of the salty sea danced
in the air.
I could feel the warm wind wrap around me
like a soft blanket as it
whistled in my ear.
The damp sand squished
in between my painted toes.
The smiling sun shone brightly in the
vibrant blue sky.
The seagulls squawked
as they flew overhead
on the lookout for food.

I could see a dark cloud
heading towards me.
The once gentle wind,
was now harsh and beat at me.
Sand scratched my dry eyes.
The once kind and smiling sun,
was hidden behind a fierce storm cloud
like it was being held hostage.
The smell of rain had a strong presence.

I dashed across the parking lot
and hopped in the car.
As my mom drove away
the driving rain pounded on the windows.
And I thought to myself
what a sad end
to such a beautiful day.

Ms. P: Camille, great job! There are so many wonderful details and sounds in this poem!

Camille: Thanks.

Ms. P: Right in the first line you have some nice alliteration with the letter "s"—it immediately creates the sound of the ocean while it describes the smell. Very clever! *(We had talked about the uses of alliteration in a mini-lesson. I star the line.)*

Camille: Yes, I wanted it to sound like the waves.

Ms. P: Great thinking. And I love this: "the warm wind wrapped" and then "whistled." That's really sophisticated, Camille—spreading out the alliteration so it echoes. You do it again below, with "squished" and "squawked." *(I star the lines.)*

Camille: That just kind of happened by coincidence.

Ms. P: Well, it still counts. You have personification throughout the poem: the "sea danced," "the smiling sun," "the wind . . . beat at me"—and similes, too: "like a soft blanket" and in the second stanza, "like it was being held hostage." Really great. And speaking of stanzas, I like how you started a new stanza when the action changed. Perfect spot for it.

> *By praising her "choices," I'm emphasizing that the poet has control over all of these techniques, even if the words and form spring naturally.*

Camille: Thanks.

Ms. P: Let's first take a look at a couple spots where you could sharpen the detail. Take this line, for example: "in between my painted toes." You had a good impulse to mention the toes were painted, but now I'm wanting to see a color.

Camille: Well, I had red at first, but it sounded like too many words: "my red painted toes." Then I thought it was weird to say "my red toes." So I just dropped it.

Ms. P: How about just "my red toenails"? No, that's not exactly right—how about, "my red-tipped toes"? Then you get some extra alliteration as well. The idea of "sand between my toes" is a bit of a cliché, so naming the color breaks it up somewhat.

> *I'm giving her a free line, but also showing her that I stab around for phrases just like she does.*

Camille: Okay. That sounds good. *(She writes the phrase in the margins.)*

Ms. P: Another spot is at the end of the first stanza, where you say seagulls looked for "food." What exactly was it?

Camille: I don't know. Whatever seagulls eat. Anything people drop.

Ms. P: Right—it's your job to figure out what that might be and name it. You don't have to list every single thing; you could name only one or two foods. Imagine it and think about it. *(I circle "food.")*

Camille: Okay.

Ms. P: I'm going to show you two more places like that to think about, and then I'll let you work on your own. Second stanza, second line: "heading towards me." Here's a spot where you could really use a powerful verb, like you do in other places in the poem. Maybe you want to try more personification. It's a place where you really have a chance to use something startling and you don't want to waste it. *(I circle the line.)* Do you understand what I'm suggesting?

Camille: I think so.

Ms. P: Look at your first two verbs: the smell of the sea "danced" and the wind "whistled." You didn't say "hung" or "blew." See what I mean?

Camille: Yes, okay.

Ms. P: Now look at the line "The smell of rain had a strong presence." Same idea there—it's a chance to use a surprising simile or an interesting descriptive phrase. *(I circle this line too.)* Work on those three spots and I'll check back.

Camille: Okay.

When I visit Camille the next day, she's made a number of revisions to her draft:

A Day at the Beach

The smell of the salty sea danced
in the air.
I could feel the warm wind wrap around me
like a soft blanket as it
whistled in my ear.
The damp sand squished
in between my red-tipped toes.
The smiling sun shone brightly in the
vibrant blue sky.
The seagulls squawked
as they flew overhead
on the lookout for half-eaten
French fries or pretzels.

I could see a dark cloud
billowing towards me.
The once gentle wind,
was now harsh and beat at me.
Sand scratched my dry eyes.
The once kind and smiling sun,
was hidden behind a fierce storm cloud

like it was being held hostage.
The smell of rain permeated the air.
I dashed across the parking lot
and hopped in the car.
As my mom drove away
the driving rain pounded on the windows.
And I thought to myself
what a sad end
to such a beautiful day.

Ms. P: Good work, Camille. The parts you revised are much stronger, especially the half-eaten French fries and pretzels! I can really envision those gulls!

Camille: Thanks.

Ms. P: Now, let's think about the ending. You have a whole poem full of specific sensory details, and then you end it with a few vague words like "sad" and "beautiful." The thought is a good one—that something enjoyable and beautiful has come to an end—but to spell it out like that weakens the poem, and the rest of the poem is so rich it deserves a strong ending. Does that make sense?

Camille: I think so. But I really didn't know how else to end it. It's one thing to think of description, but it's another to say something at the end.

Ms. P: That's the truth, Camille! I go through this all the time too. All poets do. Try this: stay in the moment. Don't pull back into some kind of commentary. The last detail you have is the rain pounding on the windows. Stay there.

Camille: Okay . . . but what then?

Ms. P: Well, see if you can find something in that image. Maybe expand it into a simile. Ask yourself, what else pounds? What can you compare the rain pounding to? Think about it.

Camille: I'll try.

> *Tone here is important—I'm chiding her a bit, almost teasing her that she took the easy way out of the poem. It means that I know she is capable of pushing herself more; I know she has the skill required to successfully end the poem. In no way does my tone ever indicate that I doubt her ability. On the contrary, it affirms it.*

When I check back, she has come up with this ending:

As my mom drove away
the driving rain pounded on the windows,
like a stampede chasing away
the gorgeous day.

Ms. P: Excellent idea, Camille! The stampede is wonderful! Now, just make it a stampede of something specific: cows, buffalo, horses, sheep—

Camille: Definitely horses. *(The obvious choice, but good enough.)*

Ms. P:	All right, one last revision, and I'm going to help you with it right now. Let's look at your line breaks.
Camille:	Okay.
Ms. P:	Remember the guidelines about line breaks?
Camille:	Um . . . they should be in a normal spot in the sentence . . .
Ms. P:	Right, and each line should have . . . what in it?
Camille:	Oh, something interesting.
Ms. P:	Or meaningful or important. Right. Let's take a look at your first two lines. The first is good, but the second doesn't really give us much. One easy way to fix it is simply bump "danced" down to the next line. The first line still has that interesting salty smell, and now the second line has a surprise in it with "danced." See the effect?
Camille:	Oh, yes, okay.
Ms. P:	I'm going to just put a few slashes in to strengthen some other line breaks, and cut a few words. Look at this line here—"The smiling sun shone brightly in the." See how "in the" is just hanging on the end there with no real purpose?
Camille:	Yes. It should go down.
Ms. P:	Right. It feels really choppy and disjointed to the reader. That's what I mean by breaking the line in the "normal" or natural breaks in a sentence.

I draw more slashes where I think better line breaks would be. I also cross out some unnecessary commas and repetitive words. I restrain myself from rewriting too much of the poem.

A Day at the Beach

The smell of the salty sea/ danced
in the air.
~~I could feel~~ The warm wind wrapped around me
like a soft blanket/ as it
whistled in my ear.
The damp sand squished
in between my ~~red toenails~~ red-tipped toes.
The smiling sun shone brightly/ in the
vibrant blue sky.
The seagulls squawked
as they flew overhead
on the lookout for half-eaten
French fries or pretzels.

I could see a dark cloud
billowing towards me.

The once gentle wind, **/no comma**
was now harsh and beat at me.
Sand scratched my dry eyes.
The once kind and smiling sun, **/no comma**
was hidden behind a fierce storm cloud
like it was being held hostage.
The smell of rain permeated the air.
I dashed across the parking lot
and hopped in the car.
As my mom drove ~~away~~ off
~~the driving~~ rain pounded on the windows,
like a stampede chasing away
the gorgeous day.

Ms. P: There. Try that out, and as you're retyping, feel free to make any other revisions that come to mind. Then hand it in.

Camille: Okay. Thanks!

Ms. P: You did an excellent job on this one.

I could spend more time helping Camille revise more details and weak verbs, but it would be too much, I think. Camille did push herself, and in future poems I can pick up where we left off in this assignment and challenge her even more. Her final draft reads:

A Day at the Beach

The smell of the salty sea
danced in the air.
The warm wind wrapped around me
like a soft blanket
as it whistled in my ear.
The damp sand squished
between my red-tipped toes.
The smiling sun shone brightly
in the vibrant blue sky.
The seagulls squawked
as they flew overhead
on the lookout for half-eaten
French fries or pretzels.

I could see a dark cloud
billowing towards me.

The once gentle wind
was now harsh and beat at me.
Sand scratched my dry eyes.
The kind and smiling sun
was hidden behind a fierce storm cloud
like it was being held hostage.
The smell of rain permeated the air.
I dashed across the parking lot
and hopped in the car.
As my mom drove off,
rain pounded on the windows,
like a stampede chasing away
the gorgeous day.

Simply naming a thing can go a long way in a poem. Consider the first line of another beach poem:

Florida
The wonderful smell of the sweet flowers.

I advise the student who wrote it to name a flower or two. When he says he doesn't know any names of flowers, especially ones in Florida, I suggest that some research is in order. He could search online under "Florida beach flowers" or "Florida wildflowers" and see what he finds. And while he is revising, I add, he should change "wonderful." He rewrites the first line as follows:

Florida
The sweet smell of black-eyed susans and wild azaleas.

I stress to the students that poets—all writers, in fact—regularly research words and the names of things they don't know. Specific names, as in the example above, can be rich in sound and image.

FREE VERSE

Cutting Words

Once students have developed a poem's purpose and details, they can improve their work by cutting words. Students are often tempted to explain what they are trying to say instead of letting the images and sounds do the work. I emphasize that in poetry, images and sounds do double duty: Not only do they mean what they mean on the surface, but they suggest deeper meanings that settle into the reader's subconscious and create an overall mood. The following poem, for example, contains some interesting images, but also needs some trimming:

Autumn

Crisp leaves crackling beneath my feet,
festive, lively season.
Halloween . . . ghosts flying through the air,
witches on their skeleton-like broomsticks.
Bright green and red apples,
pies, cakes and ciders.
Warmth and goodness
overflowing the room.
Pumpkins big and fat
ready to be brought home.
Opening the cave,
and ripping out internal organs.
Mad, sad, scared, mean and happy faces,
All on my doorstep.
I love Autumn!!!

Ms. P: Kristi, you have some wonderful images here: the sound of the leaves crackling, the bright apples, the pumpkins . . . and some nice alliteration with "crisp" and "crackle." You even have assonance with "leaves," "beneath," "feet," and "season." You also have a metaphor—the "cave" of the pumpkin. Very sophisticated writing. Good work!

Kristi: Thanks!

Ms. P: What I want you to think about is what you *don't* need in the poem. You've done such a nice job with the images that you don't need to do much more by telling.

Kristi: I don't get what you're saying.

Ms. P: Well, look at the third line for example. Do you think you need to say that it's Halloween? We know that it's autumn, and in that same line you have ghosts flying through the air. See what I mean?

Kristi: Oh . . . yeah, I guess it's obvious.

Ms. P: Right. And if the clues are there, readers usually enjoy figuring things out for themselves. Now, look at another spot where you could trim some words: line seven, "Warmth and goodness." I don't think you need that line because you have images that *symbolize* warmth and goodness.

Kristi: I do?

Ms. P: Yes. Pies, cakes, and ciders are images of holidays, abundance, and a family, aren't they?

Kristi: I guess so . . .

Ms. P: Think about it—when does your family make pies and cakes in autumn?

> I think she used the alliteration and metaphor purposely, but not the assonance. It probably sounded pleasing to her ear, but she didn't know why. Giving her credit for all of it will build confidence and cultivate her awareness of assonance in the future.

Kristi: For Thanksgiving.

Ms. P: Exactly. Most readers would think that same thing. You don't have to spell it out. If you want, you could make the image of the pies, cakes, and ciders more vivid and incorporate that "warmth" idea into the image. For example, you could say "cider steaming in thick mugs" or something like that. *(She writes the line in the margin.)* Even though it's the cider that's steaming, the feeling of warmth seeps into the mood of the poem and, on a deeper level, also symbolizes the warmth of the family and friends.

Kristi: Oh. And I don't have to say that? People will just know?

Ms. P: Yes. Assume that your reader is intelligent and good at reading poetry. And even if a reader doesn't consciously get it the first time he or she reads your poem, the meaning might come through later. As long as you leave enough clues. "Steaming cider" should do it. You could do the same with the pies and cakes—make them more vivid. Give more detail—name the flavors even—and make them warm without saying the word "warm." *(I write that suggestion in the margin.)* Keep the line after it, though. Actually, whatever you add to the pies and cakes, you could have them "overflow the room."

Kristi: Okay.

Ms. P: That's what's so sophisticated about the pumpkin as a cave. Tell me, what do you think about when you think of a cave?

Kristi: Well, it's dark, quiet, scary. There's water dripping . . .

Ms. P: Right. All those ideas are automatically in the word "cave" and therefore in the mood of your poem.

Kristi: Really? Without me saying it?

Ms. P: Yes. Automatically. But it's appropriate, because those ideas are part of autumn and Halloween, aren't they?

Kristi: Yes.

Ms. P: So you've made one single word do a lot of work. That's good writing. Now, what do you think of when you hear "ripping out internal organs"?

Kristi: Um, one thing killing another—a bird or a lion or something—and then eating it.

Ms. P: Right. It's that creepy feeling again, but it's fitting for Halloween. And isn't death a part of autumn? Then you have all of those "faces"—meaning pumpkins. But aren't they the faces of autumn, too? There's sadness at the end of summer—the death of things—fear because of the longer nights and decreasing supply of food, and happiness because of the warmth of family, as you illustrated above. I'm pushing it a bit here, but I think the pumpkins show all that. And they are "all on my doorstep," which is wonderful, just wonderful. They are autumn itself on your doorstep, offering what it has to offer.

Kristi: Wow, I never knew it could mean all that. I mean, I wasn't thinking that when I wrote it.

Ms. P: It's funny—in the beginning you don't know you're doing it; it happens by accident. When you write poetry, somehow the mind taps into something smarter than yourself, and these "accidents" happen. But the more you write, the more practice you get, and you are able to do it on purpose a bit more. There are always surprises, though. The good news is, you get to take credit for them anyway.

Kristi: Okay! If you say so.

Ms. P: I do. And now, one more line I want to cut—can you guess which one?

Kristi: Um . . . it's got to be the last one.

Ms. P: Yes. Your images are so strong that the last line feels like a balloon deflating. Cut it right off and end the poem with the amazing doorstep line. *(I cross out the last line.)* The only other line you could think about is the second one—see if you can do what we've been talking about, which is to change that line from a telling line to a showing line. You have the leaves. . . . Is there any way the leaves can demonstrate "festive and lively"? Could you use a simile? *(I write "Show, don't tell" and "Simile?" in the margin.)*

Kristi: I'll try, but that seems harder.

Ms. P: It's okay if that line stays, but give it a try. And let me tighten one more spot—in line four, what if you cut "like" and just said "skeleton broomsticks"? Actually, what if you just said "skeleton sticks"?

Kristi: I like it. It sounds better with the s's. Will people know that they're broomsticks?

Ms. P: Well, you could use a verb like "fly" to make sure. But you already have fly in the line above it. . . . Maybe you could think of a different verb for "fly" in either of those lines.

Kristi: Okay, that's good. *(She writes "fly—other word" in the margin.)*

Ms. P: Speaking of the verbs, why do you have them all in the present continuous, with -ing endings?

Kristi: Um, I don't know. I just wrote it that way.

Ms. P: It's not wrong. You just might want to try the simple present and see which you like better. *(I write "Try in simple present tense.")* And think about this, too— should you break it up into stanzas? That would spread it out, slow it down, and put space between the images. Up to you. Play around on the computer and see what you like. *(I write "Stanzas?" on the top of the page.)*

> *I've given her many suggestions, but since the poem is short and the images are in place, I feel confident she can handle them.*

Kristi: Okay, maybe. I'll see.

Ms. P: You have a lot to think about, but that's because the images are so rich in the first place. Great work so far, Kristi.

Kristi: Thanks!

Kristi works for another day or so on revising, and I briefly consult with her once more about the stanzas. I fix some punctuation as I'm grading the poem. In the end, it looks like this:

Autumn

Crisp leaves crackle beneath my feet
like giant pieces of confetti.

Ghosts dash through the air;
witches fly on their skeleton sticks.

Bright green and red apples,
oozing pecan pies and pound cakes

overflow the room.
Cider steams in thick mugs.

Pumpkins big and fat
ready to be brought home.

We open the cave,
and rip out internal organs.

Mad, sad, scared, mean and happy faces
all on my doorstep.

ODE

Using Imagery to Establish Mood; Changing Clichés; Finding an Ending

Students often write about the seasons and the weather, especially for the first few poetry assignments. In the following poem, Tom's imagery is mostly interesting but it sends mixed messages about the mood. And, like Kristi's poem, Tom's will be better off without the last lines.

Ode for Snow

White as a cloud,
Fluffy as cotton candy,
The crystals piled up,
Like the presents at Christmas time.
The wet cold flakes
Sifted in the wind.
The snowmen are staring,
As the plows go by.
Sitting in a heated house,
With a hot chocolate by my side.
A new pair of clothes,
And a blanket in my hand,
I hear the slamming of sleds,
And the faint echo of shoveling.
The sky is getting gray,
And more snow is coming,
So I should bundle up because,
There is going to be a blizzard.

Ms. P: Tom, you have some really nice lines here, and details for almost all the senses, I think.

Tom: Yeah, I tried to do that—the hot cocoa is both a taste and a smell, I figured.

Ms. P: Let's look at all your images. The poem is an ode, so we can assume you are praising snow, correct?

Tom: Yes.

Ms. P: Okay. You say it is white and fluffy, and "like the presents at Christmas time," which is a great simile by the way, because it does double duty—it describes the sight of the snowflakes piling up, and it also reminds the reader that Christmas comes during the winter. All of these images create a joyful mood, right?

Tom: Yes.

Ms. P: Then we have the snowmen staring, which is a great detail to focus on, and great alliteration, but it is a bit ambiguous—the staring, I mean. The snowmen are not smiling or waving; they're staring. It could go either way, good or bad. The snowmen could be just peaceful, or evil. We don't know.

Tom: Evil snowmen—that's a good one. So what's the problem?

Ms. P: Well, the reader won't know how to feel. Right after that, we have the speaker safe in a heated house with a blanket and cocoa. Then we have "the slamming of sleds" which is absolutely wonderful for its description and alliteration. But "slamming" is a bit violent, right? It could be fun or it could be dangerous.

Tom: Okay . . .

Ms. P: But the clincher on the strange mood is the ending—the sky is getting gray, a blizzard is coming, the speaker needs to bundle up, meaning he is not as safe as we thought. See how it turns somewhat foreboding at the end, and it makes the snowmen and the sleds slamming seem even more ominous?

Tom: Yes. I wanted to make it seem like snow is out of our control. But still fun.

Ms. P: I thought so. First, I think you should cut the last two lines. Saying the sky is gray and more snow is coming is enough.

Tom: Okay. *(He crosses out the last two lines.)*

Ms. P: But ending with the gray sky is still very foreboding.

Tom: What else could I use though?

Ms. P: Well, maybe you don't have to think of something new. Maybe you could move around what you already have. Try this: Print out four copies of the poem—one using the "presents" at the end, one with the snowmen at the end, one with the blanket, and one with the shoveling. Don't simply cut and paste—toy around with each draft so it makes sense. Then see what each effect is. Maybe you'll like one as an ending. Remember what you told me—you want the idea of the poem to be that we can't control snow but it is still fun. See if you can find an image that fits that. *(I circle the four images I mentioned, and write "Can't control snow, but fun" in the margin and star it.)*

Tom: Okay.

When I check back, Tom has the four drafts in front of him.

1. Ode for Snow

White as a cloud,
Fluffy as cotton candy,
The wet cold flakes
Sifted in the wind.
The snowmen are staring,
As the plows go by.
Sitting in a heated house,
With a hot chocolate by my side.
A new pair of clothes,
And a blanket in my hand,
I hear the slamming of sleds,
And the faint echo of shoveling.
The sky is getting gray,
And more snow is coming.
The crystals piled up,
Like the presents at Christmas time.

2. Ode for Snow

White as a cloud,
Fluffy as cotton candy,
The crystals piled up,
Like the presents at Christmas time.
The wet cold flakes
Sifted in the wind.
Sitting in a heated house,
With a hot chocolate by my side.
A new pair of clothes,
And a blanket in my hand,
I hear the slamming of sleds,
And the faint echo of shoveling.
The sky is getting gray,
And more snow is coming.
The snowmen are staring,
As the plows go by.

3. Ode for Snow

White as a cloud,
Fluffy as cotton candy,
The crystals piled up,
Like the presents at Christmas time.
The wet cold flakes
Sifted in the wind.
The snowmen are staring,
As the plows go by.
I hear the slamming of sleds,
And the faint echo of shoveling.
The sky is getting gray,
And more snow is coming,
I am sitting in a heated house,
With a hot chocolate by my side.
A new pair of clothes,
And a blanket in my hand.

4. Ode for Snow

White as a cloud,
Fluffy as cotton candy,
The crystals piled up,
Like the presents at Christmas time.
The wet cold flakes
Sifted in the wind.
The snowmen are staring,
As the plows go by.
Sitting in a heated house,
With a hot chocolate by my side.
A new pair of clothes,
And a blanket in my hand,
The sky is getting gray,
And more snow is coming.
I hear the slamming of sleds,
And the faint echo of shoveling.

Ms. P: Good work, Tom. What do you think?

Tom: Well, I think number one and three are kind of boring at the end, like who cares if I have a blanket?

Ms. P: I agree! Great instincts. What else?

Tom: I like number four and number two, because it seems like the snow will win out. Do you know what I mean?

Ms. P: I do. It's the last image—people shoveling or the snowmen watching the plows.

Tom: The only problem with the snowmen is that they do seem kind of scary. Once you said that, I could see it. They're a little weird just staring there.

I'm hoping for the snowmen ending, but I don't want to tell him what to do here.

Ms. P: Well, they don't have to stare. You could have them making another face.

Tom: How about "smiling"?

Ms. P: I think that's perfect—they're happy that more snow is coming and they're almost teasing the plow operators.

Tom: Yeah.

Ms. P: Excellent. Instead of using the present continuous tense in that line, though, I'd just use the present. Do you know what I mean?

Tom: Um . . .

Ms. P: The present continuous is when you use "are" and "-ing." *(I underline the verb.)* It means it's happening right now. But it also feels a bit temporary. How could you change it to the regular, simple present tense?

Tom: "Smile"?

Ms. P: Right. That seems more permanent, don't you think? "The snowmen smile/as the plows go by."

Tom: Yes. Like they're going to be there a while.

Ms. P: Exactly. Now, there is one new part in number one that I like.

Tom: What's that?

Ms. P: The first four lines together the way they are. It sounds better than having the lines about the Christmas presents right in the middle there.

Tom: Should I cut the presents?

Ms. P: No, no—it's a strong simile, as I told you before. Maybe just put them as lines five and six. *(I take draft number three, circle the "Christmas" lines, and draw an arrow down.)*

Tom: Okay.

Ms. P: I'm also going to show you a trick for the first two lines. To say "white as a cloud" and "fluffy as cotton candy" is a bit clichéd, don't you think? I mean if I said to a class, "What's white?" or "What's fluffy?" don't you think those would be the first answers?

Tom: I guess so. Should I change them?

Ms. P: Well, if anything pops in your head, go for it. But what we could do for now is just tighten those lines up to metaphors instead of similes.

Tom: What does that mean?

Ms. P: Well, what two words make a simile?

Tom: Uh . . . "like" and "as"?

Ms. P: Right. What if we took out "as" and made up a term like "cloud-white"?

Tom: You can do that?

Ms. P: Sure. Poets do it all the time. There's one poet in particular who is a master at it— Seamus Heaney. Remember when we read his poem "The Rainstick" and it had all those invented hyphenated words?

Tom: I think so. Was that the one about the guy playing with his kids' toy?

Ms. P: Basically, yes. I'll give you another copy to look at. What if you had as your first line, "Cloud-white cotton candy," and then, "The wet cold flakes / Sifted in the wind." That way, the first line would be a describing phrase for "flakes."

Tom: It sounds good, too.

Ms. P: Yes, since we squished it together we have some nice alliteration. *(I write the line and cross out the old lines.)* Okay, there are two important tasks left here.

Tom: What?

Ms. P: I want you to go through the poem and highlight all the verbs. You should notice something.

Tom: Really? Oh—that I switch from past to present?

Ms. P: Right. Choose one and keep it. Then examine every comma. Imagine your poem in sentences. If you wouldn't normally use the comma in the sentence, don't use it in the poem. Just because it's the end of a line doesn't mean it should have a comma.

Tom: Okay.

Ms. P: Then hand it in. I really like this one, Tom. Good work.

Tom: Thanks.

> *The first two lines are clichés, but I don't want to send him back to the drawing board on his own at this point. The main lesson for this assignment was finding an ending.*

I fix some lingering punctuation mistakes after Tom hands the poem in. The final copy reads:

Ode for Snow

Cloud-white cotton candy,
The wet cold flakes
Sift in the wind.
The crystals pile up
Like the presents at Christmas time.
Sitting in a heated house
With a hot chocolate by my side,
A new pair of clothes,
And a blanket in my hand,
I hear the slamming of sleds,
And the faint echo of shoveling.
The sky is getting gray,
And more snow is coming.
The snowmen smile
As the plows go by.

RHYMED POEM

Revising Forced Rhymes

Novice poets tend to use predictable or contrived rhyming, so in mini-lessons, I emphasize that poets must push themselves to find rhymes that make sense, seem natural, and are interesting or even a little bit surprising. Using a plethora of examples helps convince them to strive beyond the easiest rhymes that pop into their heads. In addition, I advocate near-rhymes and enjambment in order to make the rhyming more natural. The next example is a wonderful poem except for the rhyming in the first four lines. The poem begins:

Summer Days

Summer days are really odd,
can you feel the heat?
Like they are sent to us from God.
I can feel the sun beat
down on me . . .

Ms. P: Dave, this poem is so clever and well-done! I absolutely love the near rhymes and the line breaks you used in order to make the rhyming flow naturally. Very sophisticated.

Dave: Thanks.

Ms. P: The only part that feels like you forced the rhyme is in the beginning. Why is the heat odd? And God doesn't appear in the rest of the poem, so why mention God in the beginning?

> *Like many beginning poets, he was hoping he could just get away with it.*

Dave: I know. I couldn't think of anything else.

Ms. P: Well, I could tell that you couldn't, and that's not a thought you want your reader to have. The rest of the rhyming is so well-done; the poem deserves a strong beginning. Try this: use the word "days" and look up some rhymes for it. It's an important word in the poem, and even though you have external rhyming throughout, there's no rule that you can't have a little internal rhyme as well. See if anything jumps out at you for a revision of the first and third lines. You may or may not have to revise the second and fourth lines to make it all fit, but try to keep the rhymes intact in the second and fourth lines since the fourth line enjambs with the fifth. Do you know what I mean?

> *I circle "odd" and "God" and write "rhyme with 'days'?" Students normally wouldn't think of internally rhyming. For them, internal rhyme is usually just a happy accident. However, picking a word from what the student has already written and sending him to the rhyming dictionary with it can often open the imagination to new possibilities. Plus, it will sound pleasing.*

Dave: Yes. Okay, I'll try it.

His revised stanza:

Summer Days

*On summer days I feel the craze
of hot and humid heat.
I run for cover under the blaze,
feeling the relentless sun beat
down on me . . .*

Ms. P: Excellent, Dave! I think these rhymes fit better, and the internal rhyme makes the poem even more musical. But since your meter is nicely offbeat, the rhyming doesn't feel singsongy, like a nursery rhyme. Do you understand?

Dave: Yes. I purposely tried not to use "haze," since I figured you would say that was the obvious choice.

Ms. P: Now you're thinking like a poet! In the penultimate—that means second-to-last—line, you repeat the word "heat." Maybe you could replace it with "haze," and that way you wouldn't have "heat" twice, and you would have a nice echo of these beginning rhymes. What do you think?

Dave: Okay, yeah. Thanks.

Ms. P: Great work on this one. Hand it in when you're done.

Here is Dave's final poem:

Summer Days

On summer days I feel the craze
of hot and humid heat.
I run for cover under the blaze,
feeling the relentless sun beat
down on me as if it's walking
on me. If the sun were alive
I could just imagine it mocking
us, how we used to be cool without bee hives
or sweat or T-shirts.
What I hate is the struggle, the dirt,
the haze, the ticks in my hair.
That's why I have central air.

The varied meter is wonderful, but the poem could be tidied up a bit. But since I know well how hard it is to write natural-sounding formal poetry, I am pleased with Dave's attempt and his progress with rhyming.

As with all other genres, I make sure when talking to students about their poems that I maintain a tone of confident expectation. I try to convey that with effort, they can create meaningful poems. In middle school, students generally aren't as intimidated by poetry as adults can be; they may moan about the work it takes to use rhyme and meter effectively, but underneath it all they still love sound and rhythm. After all, they are only a few years removed from the beloved nursery rhymes of childhood and can still feel them like the familiar rhythms of a heartbeat. The idea of this pulse is my underlying message all year—that whether we realize it or not, our lives and very beings are made of words, and that by writing them as clearly and honestly as possible, we both reveal and create ourselves.

Conference Techniques Quick Reference

GENERAL

- Find places in the writing that deserve praise, and praise them specifically and genuinely.
- Dictate back the students' actual spoken words; write down anything usable the student says.
- Soften criticism with terms like "a bit," "somewhat," or "a little," without backing away from the issue.
- Avoid talk, even praise, of talent.
- Let students know when they know more about a hobby, place, sport, or area of study than you.
- Repeatedly point out what "real" writers do and acknowledge when students employ the habits of "real" writers. Always treat students as "real" writers and refer to them as such.
- Break up instruction with questions or by having the student list, underline, highlight, circle, checkmark, count, or read aloud.
- Give an obvious example to illustrate a point and then say: "Don't use that, but try something like that. You'll come up with something better."
- Don't dumb down literary terms; instead, phrase them so that the student will understand their meaning through context.

NOTHING TO WRITE

- Connect to sample reading.
- Review the Topics for Writing.
- Ask the student to make short lists; you name the categories.
- Get the student talking—find an emotional connection to a topic.

DETAILS

- List five senses.
- Ask about the weather and/or the light in that moment.
- Have the student relive the experience if possible.
- Have the student freewrite about the memory and highlight any details; from there list more.
- Require a specific number of details or a certain length in freewriting.
- Remind the student there are no "wrong" details, only ones that will or won't be used.
- Underline "telling" sentences and convert to showing; tell the student not to use the "telling" word but to make sure, through description, the reader will be thinking it.
- Have the student convert linking verbs to action verbs.
- Get the student talking—find the emotional connection.
- Ask about any existing details to find additional or more specific details. For example, for sight details, ask about colors; for sounds, onomatopoeia.

THEME

- Look for a hint of a theme in the student's details, phrasing, and plot.
- Have the student begin a sentence with "I learned," "I realized," or "I knew then."
- Ask the student, "How did you change from this experience?"
- Ask, "How did you feel after this experience?" Then ask, "Why?"
- Say: "It's not just about [the student's topic], it's about your life. [The topic] is a part of your life, don't you think?"

ORGANIZATION

Before students write:

- Prevent disorganization by giving detailed instructions on what types of organizational structure work best for each genre.
- Draw attention to organizational possibilities by having students analyze sample essays for each genre.

During and after writing:

- Check the student's prewriting.
- Help the student sort out a few main ideas, make an outline, and cut the rest.
- Have the student cut the draft into pieces with scissors, then pile the ideas in order, or tape them to a new page, or save them in envelopes.
- Have the student assign a different highlighting color to each main idea, and then highlight the entire essay in those colors.

OTHER CONCLUSIONS/CLINCHERS

- Keep the student grounded in the specific; don't let him pull back into generalities. (Not the same as using a "general statement of truth" to recapitulate the essay's theme.)
- Look for a specific image in the paper that can be saved for the end or reused at the end, this time symbolically.
- Revisit the examples in the piece and dig deeper; the new ideas can be incorporated in the conclusion.
- Suggest a specific sentence construction (like "if . . . then" or "not only . . . but also"); even start the sentence for the student, and let her fill in the rest.

INTRODUCTION

- Look for the best moment of description or tension, start there, and use a flashback to fill in.
- Have the student examine the first paragraphs in an anthology of short stories.

- Have a file or binder of finished essays and have the student examine those introductions.
- Have "Ways to Start an Essay" posted in the classroom or highlighted in the students' notebooks and refer to it often.
- Look for where the bulk of the essay's information appears, or where the student's interest in the topic is most clear, and see if one of the approaches can be used in relation to that.
- Have the student write two or even three introductions and analyze them.

LANGUAGE

- Check for banned words.
- Give the student one or two alternatives to a banned or weak word, then ask her to add a third and choose from among them.
- Constantly direct the student toward the sensory details.
- Help the student eradicate linking verbs.
- Remind the student not to start sentences the same way in the same paragraph.
- Direct the student to sources (posters, thesauri, sample essays or poems, and so on) for ideas.
- Check for words like "something," "someone," "somewhere," and so on. Should these be named?
- Look for two or more words whose meaning can be conveyed in one word.
- Look for verb-adverb combinations whose meanings can be conveyed in single, stronger verbs.
- Look for verb-preposition combinations.
- Pare large chunks of passive voice by looking for the doers of the actions.

TITLES

- Give the student key words from her piece that symbolize or indicate the theme and topic. Have her mix and match them to form titles.
- Remind the student of his thesis.
- Search for vital information in the piece that can be extracted to form the title (for example, a place name).

THESIS

- Have the student explain in her own words how she feels about a topic. Repeat it back to her, and have her take notes.
- Give the student key phrases of a potential thesis (particular to his topic and opinion) and let him piece the sentence together.

REVISING POETRY

- Push for the most specific detail possible.
- Trim any words that can be trimmed.
- Look for any unconsciously repeated words and change or cut.
- Envision the poem in another form (stanzas or no stanzas) and suggest the student play with the lines on a computer and observe the effect.
- Examine the line breaks. The student can keep to the rule of a line being (1) meaningful and (2) interesting, or she can break it somewhere unexpected for effect. Suggest places where the student can experiment with line breaks on the computer.

ENDING A POEM

- Advise student to stay in the moment.
- Advise student to try a simile.
- Advise student to look at the lines preceding the weak ending: is there anything there that can be expanded into a better ending?
- Can the final lines simply be cut and earlier lines used as an ending?
- Is there an overarching image in the poem, or a small detail, that can be used in an interesting way at the end?
- Could repetition be used?

Professional References

Atwell, Nancie. *In the Middle: New Understandings About Writing, Reading, and Learning.* 2nd ed. Portsmouth, NH: Boynton/Cook Publishers, 1998.

ADOLESCENT LITERATURE/MOVIES REFERRED TO IN THE CONFERENCES

Woodsong by Gary Paulsen

"The Green Gulch" by Loren Eiseley

The Outsiders by S.E. Hinton

"The Color of Friendship" directed by Kevin Hooks

"A Worn Path" by Eudora Welty

"All Summer in a Day" by Ray Bradbury

"Sonic Boom" by John Updike